LAST SUNSET

by the same author

NOVELS

A NECESSARY END

LIVE TILL TOMORROW

LAST SUNSET

STEPHEN HARPER

COLLINS
St James's Place, London
1978

William Collins Sons & Co Ltd
London · Glasgow · Sydney · Auckland
Toronto · Johannesburg

HERTFORDSHIRE
LIBRARY SERVICE

953.35

8805271

First published 1978
© Stephen Harper 1978

ISBN 0 00 216458 2

Set in Plantin
Made and Printed in Great Britain by
William Collins Sons & Co Ltd Glasgow

Contents

Illustrations

'I have visited every part of Arabia and the tribes in the neighbourhood of Aden are more treacherous and false than any other. Justice and right thinking is unknown to them. They are a people incapable of estimating the value of good government'

COMMANDER STAFFORD HAINES, *founder of Aden Colony, in a letter to the East India Company in Bombay in 1851.*

'It is a paradox of this anti-Colonial era that if Britain's Empire were suddenly to relinquish its appanages in the Persian Gulf, NATO and the Free World might collapse'

C. L. SULZBERGER, *New York Times, 1957.*

Author's Preface

There was no flag ceremony on 29 November 1967 as a Wasp helicopter of a Royal Marines rearguard scurried towards the safety of a Royal Navy evacuation fleet of twenty-four ships anchored off Aden.

The final British redoubt was the twelfth 'brown' of a desert golf course, marked out as a helicopter pad, surrounded by sandbag gun positions.

The rearguard commander, Lieutenant Commander Dai Morgan, was hardly airborne in the last helicopter pick-up before the black, white and red starred flag of the Marxist National Liberation Front fluttered over the deserted clubhouse, daubed 'Fort Alamo' in crudely painted letters.

Barely quarter of a century before its premeditated withdrawal from East of Suez, Britain was an accepted equal partner with America and Russia in leadership of the victorious powers of World War Two. The sun went down on the vast empire 'on which the sun never set' during the years a war baby grew to manhood. Burma, the first British possession to become independent, and Aden, among the last, were the only former British territories to reject a continuing relationship with Britain as members of the Commonwealth. Both suffered cruelly from outside intervention in the closing years.

At the end of World War Two British paramountcy in the Middle East was more formidable than it had ever been. Its pillars collapsed like skittles after the end of the British mandate in Palestine in 1948, a withdrawal that left Arab and Jew to seek an armed solution still no nearer after four major wars. Soon after the first Arab defeat in 1948 a newly outward-looking Soviet Union rowed back from initial early recognition of Israel and settled on a cynical mischief-making policy of all-out backing for Arab aspirations. British power declined rapidly as revolutionary regimes took over in Egypt, Iraq, the Sudan and Libya. British influence was ousted even from King Hussein's Jordan, a state created by Britain at the Versailles Peace Conference. It lingered on only in the backwaters of the Persian Gulf and Aden, the only British colony in the Arab world.

Three years before the sneak-out from the Aden fortress, British forces had won the last colonial campaign in the great

Empire's long history of battle. It was fought with armour, artillery and bombing planes along the wild Yemen frontier. It demonstrated Britain's will to rule in the way rebellious tribesmen were deemed to understand best. It showed that Britain could stay in those parts as long as she chose.

A change of government in London soon afterwards brought a total reversal of policy. Britain chose to leave Aden and other bases East of Suez, lock, stock and barrel.

As the sun went down in a huge ball of red over the Arabian Sea that November evening of 1967, most of the tribal rulers of the desert hinterland, with whose forebears Britain had signed treaties of perpetual protection, had already bleated betrayal and fled their palaces fearful of Marxist-led mobs. Britain left behind many other Arabs with a greater feeling of let-down – humbler men who had worked to improve the lot of their own people as officials of a benevolent colonialism. For most of them there was no escape.

It was, in many ways, a forerunner for a later evacuation of Western power and influence. Something similar on a vastly greater human scale happened in Saigon almost a decade later. Aden was Britain's Vietnam.

Within days Aden dropped right out of newspaper headlines. Within months it was as much a part of obscure history as the Indian Mutiny and other events best forgotten. Continued withdrawals from the developing oil sheikdoms of the Gulf over the next four years were hardly noticed at all.

A decade later the Gulf is a wonderland of excessive wealth, and Aden is a land of abject poverty rating rare mention in the outside world only as a refuge for hijackers of airliners allowed to land nowhere else. History has turned full circle. Only the scale of piracy has changed. The offshore plundering of an Indian trading ship that served as a pretence for Britain to establish an Imperial Base at Aden in 1839 has wider application today. It is now a training base and refuge for international terrorists.

There were two infinitely more serious consequences of Britain's abandonment of Aden.

The Soviet Union moved quickly to fill the power vacuum and rapidly built up a huge naval capability in the Indian Ocean. Warships of the Soviet Navy now dominate the oil tanker lanes from the Persian Gulf to Europe and America.

The traditional rulers of the oil-rich sheikdoms, suddenly

vulnerable, were cajoled by revolutionary neighbour states first into funding 'the battle for Arab rights in Palestine', then to the use of oil as a weapon against Israel's alleged supporters in the West. Bereft of the old protective alliances with Britain that had so recently saved Kuwait from absorption into revolutionary Iraq, they had no choice.

The capitalist world of the West, Britain most of all, still totters economically from the decision of the Arab kings and sheiks to give in to longstanding demands for use of the Arabs' ultimate weapon – oil.

It has been left to America, emerging from its agonizing re-appraisal of foreign and defence policies, to begin to redress the balance, a process becoming discernible in Cairo and other Arab capitals.

This book is an attempt to record an Englishman's impression of the last twenty years of British imperial power in the place it really ended. The few far-flung islands still under the British flag are mere residues of that nineteenth-century British global supremacy. None of them, not even the Rock of Gibraltar, have any meaning today in terms of power. They are history's leftovers.

The writer was present as a newspaper correspondent at most key developments in Arabia over that period. He also lived for eighteen months in Moscow around the critical period of the 1962 Cuban confrontation, chrysalis of the present Soviet global posture.

His is a British point of view but is, he hopes, informed by some sympathy for Arab aspirations.

It is not apologetic. The overall record warrants more pride than shame in days when trade and fair dealing were protected by the Union Jack.

PART ONE

1 Coaling Station

The British capture of Aden in 1839 was intended to serve firm notice of Britain's readiness to respond energetically to designs on India by the main imperial rival, France. The French were supporting the ambitious Egyptian Pasha, Mohamed Ali, who had proclaimed independence from Constantinople and brought the greater part of Arabia under his rule. A French-trained Egyptian army was marching on Islam's holiest city, Mecca. Elements of it occupied the coastal littoral of Yemen little more than a hundred miles from Aden.

The British Foreign Secretary, Lord Palmerston, was convinced that Mohamed Ali, celebrated around Bedouin camp fires for his salty treacheries and daring, was secretly conspiring with Russian agents as well as using the French. Palmerston believed that Mohamed Ali, scion of a mercenary family from Albania, sought to establish an Arabian Kingdom over 'all of the countries of which Arabic is the language'. Such a stabilizing control of an endemically lawless area was welcome to British merchants in Alexandria, Baghdad and Bombay. But Palmerston would not have it. 'There's no harm in such a thing in itself,' he said dismissively. 'But as it would necessarily imply the dismemberment of Turkey we cannot agree to it.'

About the same time, George Eden, Earl of Auckland, was writing to the would-be Caliph of Cairo to thank him for facilitating mail services overland from the Euphrates to the Bosphorous through a region where Mohamed Ali's armies were fighting the old Ottoman masters. He wrote from the Governor-General's office in Calcutta, 'Only a potentate of Your Excellency's liberal and enlightened mind can appreciate the advantage of free and general intercourse'.

Palmerston was mesmerized by the covetous eyes Russia fixed on Britain's commercial empire in India, later to become the Indian Empire, brightest jewel in the British Imperial Crown, and a key factor in providing military manpower East of Suez. The Czar's agents were known to be conspiring with both Mohamed Ali and his enemies the Turks, and a Prussian general named Von Moltke was preparing an army to restore Ottoman authority over Syria, where Mohamed Ali's son, Ibrahim, was governor.

The Ottoman Empire, a buffer zone of enervating sloth stretching across the landmass between India and the vigorous peoples to the north and west, was at last disintegrating. Napoleon's occupation of Egypt had first broken the unwritten pact of non-intervention in this vast zone. Further French intrigues in fostering the ambitions of Mohamed Ali prompted Britain to end it.

The annexation of Aden was soon followed by undisputed British domination of the Persian Gulf under forms of suzerainty less forthright than the total sovereignty proclaimed over Aden, but none the less potent. The Sultan of Muscat urged Britain to block Egyptian expansion by occupying Bahrein Island and the desert oasis of Buraimi. It was, instead, done more subtly through a series of treaties of protection to the petty rulers of the coastal littoral inside the Gulf. These documents effectively kept all other powers from meddling in the area while necessitating a British military presence that was to become widely acclaimed by liberals throughout the civilized world for its police actions against piracy and the slave trade.

It was to be many years before strategic considerations governed by the defence of India were to give way to more pressing problems of safeguarding the lifeblood of twentieth-century industrial power in Britain, itself, and in the entire western world. The significance of the black viscous liquid that lay in desert pools, useful only in lanterns and to caulk the timbers of sailing dhows, was to become apparent many decades later.

The formal British occupation of Aden in 1839 came forty years after the first British military intervention in the area. At the turn of the century a three-man Secret Committee of the Court of Directors of the East India Company had foreshadowed official government policy. With the assent of the Lords Commissioners of the Admiralty, ships and transports of the Royal Navy landed the company's employee, Lieutenant-Colonel J. Murray, with a detachment of the company's Indian sepoys, on the uninhabited island of Perim on 3 May 1799.

Colonel Murray's orders were to survey the island for gun positions that would command the narrow Bab al-Mandeb straits linking the Red Sea with the Indian Ocean. From Perim, a mile off the coast of Yemen, the African coast looms twelve miles away through a permanent heat haze. The company was worried lest Napoleon, briefly in occupation of Egypt, might send warships from bases at Suez to plunder their richly laden ships from India.

Water shortage prevented sustained occupation of the barren island. Within a year the tiny garrison withdrew to the comparative lushness of Aden in the Southern Arabian sultanate of Lahej. The Sultan of Lahej was friendly, and in need of a powerful ally to help maintain independence against a recurrence of Yemen expansionism.

He suggested that the British should set up a trading settlement in Aden, twenty-four miles from his capital. Murray passed the idea and the invitation to his superiors in Bombay, but the Council of Bombay passed it up and called Murray and his entire force back to Bombay in 1801. The order came from executives of a company trading under royal charter. Apart from the triumvirate of the Secret Committee, the East India Company's directors were concerned more with trading profits than political or strategic ploys. They were glad to wind up the expenses of an expedition, launched without their knowledge, purely in the political interest.

Only a year later, in 1802, Sultan Ahmed of Lahej signed a trade agreement with the East India Company during a visit by Commodore Sir Home Popham of the Royal Navy. It was merely a diplomatic courtesy, a statement of kindly intent, making no mention of a British settlement at Aden. That idea was already forgotten in Bombay. Sultan Ahmed repeated his desire to have a British trading settlement at Aden to a young surveyor of the company's Bombay Marine, a Lieutenant Haines, who was briefly in Aden in 1820.

Haines visited Aden again after a break of fifteen years. In the meantime Sultan Ahmed had died, and was succeeded by a nephew. Sultan Mahsin received Haines with the same hospitality as his uncle and spoke of his fears of Turkish conquest and his need of protection of the kind a British settlement in Aden might offer. But it was no more than dinner-table conversation.

The Bombay Council of the East India Company was brought under the control of central direction from Calcutta in 1833. The company was fighting a series of wars in India, Afghanistan, Persia and Burma – all aimed at securing British power in India. Swifter consultation with London became urgent as intrigues proliferated throughout the Middle East. Answers to recommendations put to the Government in distant London took on average twelve to eighteen months by mail around the Cape, and the land route across Mesopotamia was uncertain. Already officials were tending to become less bold in decision making, fearing for their pensions, noting some spectacular plunges from wealth and power by more eminent servants of the company who fell victim to the envy of lesser men.

Urgent mail across Egypt from Alexandria, and then by dhow to Bombay, cut the Cape time by one-third. But strong north winds made the Red Sea route impossible for eight months of the year. The invention of the coal-burning steam ship brought a prospect of regular mail packets between Suez and Bombay.

The first steamship built in Bombay, the *Hugh Lindsay*, 411 tons, sailed on her maiden voyage on 20 March 1830, and reached Aden eleven days later, and Suez on the thirty-third day out of Bombay. A year later the voyage was trimmed to twenty-two days. A year after that Commander Stafford Bettesworth Haines, of the Indian Navy (as the Bombay Marine was by then called) was ordered to make a survey of the Arabian coast to find a suitable place for a coal depot. Coal shipped around the Cape had risen as high as £20 a ton at new bunkering yards in Suez before supplies via Nile barge and camel train brought the price down to £4 a ton.

Haines, born in 1802 (the year of the courtesy trade treaty with Lahej) already knew the area well and had visited Aden twice. But the company's first choice was the island of Socotra, far out in the Indian Ocean, owned by the mainland Sultan of Mahra, who steadfastly refused to sell any of his birthright. Such a refusal, respected and admired by Haines, had not occurred to the company's merchant princes in Bombay. They had already despatched a force to occupy Socotra. However, it was quickly decimated by fever, and withdrawn.

Meanwhile Haines had continued his survey. He found Aden's tiny trade much diminished since his earlier visits. Under the wavering and capricious misrule of Sultan Mahsin it had become a village of ninety dilapidated stone buildings surrounded by clusters of banana thatch huts. It was, however, ideal for his purposes – natural defences of sheer rock faces on the landward side and harbours on both sides of the peninsula offering shelter from all prevailing winds.

He described it thus, 'The Sultan has driven away the merchants with high taxes, and it is a miserable village without trade, and but seldom visited except by passing vessels, which anchor for protection in its splendid harbour. Under British government it could become a place of the first mercantile importance'.

The ruined fortifications only needed repair. Guns lay dismounted and neglected in their former embrasures. Even the tiny waterfront was badly silted up.

Haines's recommendation for the purchase of Aden as a coaling station lay in company pending trays until news reached Bombay of the plunder of an Indian sailing ship, the *Duria Dowlat,* which had been forced aground near Aden in January 1837. Fourteen passengers were drowned, and wealthy Indian ladies among surviving Muslim pilgrims to Mecca were rudely treated. The ship was under British colours, belonged to the important Nawab of the Carnatic, and carried a valuable cargo.

Commander Haines was despatched from Bombay in the Indian Navy sloop *Coote,* ostensibly to demand reparations. His main mission was to obtain Aden by purchase for use as a coal-bunkering port. He arrived on 28 December, eleven months after the piracy of the *Duria Dowlat.* There was clear evidence of a conspiracy between the ship's handling agent in Aden and the Sultan's family to wreck the ship and loot its cargo. Some of the plunder was still on sale in the Sultan's warehouse.

Haines dealt first with the piracy question, claiming an indemnity of 12,000 Maria Theresa dollars, heavy coins, minted from silver originally mined in Bavaria, widely used as international currency in the eighteenth and nineteenth centuries, and still in use today in remote markets of Arabia. After many denials and much haggling Haines settled for the return of goods worth 8000 dollars and a promissory note for the balance.

Then he negotiated, with much less haggling, the purchase of Aden for an annual payment of 8700 dollars. But even as Haines prepared to sail for Bombay, promising to return with the first settlers in March, elderly Sultan Mahsin began to renege on his sealed agreement for the sale of the land that was to become Aden Colony. His heirs objected bitterly to the sale of any part of their birthright, and Haines had to outwit a conspiracy to kidnap him and destroy the document of sale.

These developments made the Bombay Government hesitate. Six months were wasted while officials worried over the extra expense of having to use force, and somewhat less about reactions of the other great powers to such an eventuality. They were finally spurred to action by fears that the Egyptians, then occupying the coastal areas of Yemen, might march on to Aden. For it also came to their attention that the stern Lord Palmerston, unaware of the delay caused by their indecision, had already warned Louis Napoleon to stay clear of the British sovereign territory of Aden. Once again Haines embarked in the *Coote* with an escort of thirty with orders 'to take peaceable possession of Aden'. If he found that the Egyptians had meanwhile established a garrison there he was empowered to warn Ibrahim Pasha, Governor of Yemen and nephew of Mohamed Ali, to leave British territory forthwith or face the consequences.

The *Coote* anchored in Front Bay off Crater (the English translation of Aden) on 24 October 1838 to find the Sultan's eldest son, Hamed, in defiant charge of a garrison of one hundred and fifty desert tribesmen. With them, manning fourteen cannon, were a number of Egyptians. It was never clarified whether they were military advisers under Egyptian orders or merely mercenaries, deserters from the occupation army in Yemen.

Haines and his escort stayed aboard the *Coote*. He sent back to Bombay for reinforcements and began protracted negotiations by letter with Sultan Mahsin. The Sultan's family was openly contemptuous of the British for only being able to send one ship. The Sultan's letters became increasingly insulting, finally drawing this admonition from the patient Haines, 'You write of the British Government as if you were speaking of some petty sheikdom. Undeceive yourself – they are powerful and will not be trifled with. Would you play with a lion as with a cat?'

He ordered a blockade of Aden, preventing the entry of cattle boats from Somalia and interdicting camel trains from the hinterland by salvoes from the *Coote*'s cannon. Another Indian Navy schooner, the *Mahi*, with the armed barque, *Anne Crichton*, arrived in mid-December to reinforce the blockade.

The Fadhli tribe, whose territories ran up the coast east of Aden, were bitter enemies of the ruling Abdali tribe in Lahej. They supplied wood, water and fresh fruit to the British ships and offered to join in an attack on Lahej. Haines declined their military aid, thus beginning a policy of not taking sides in tribal rivalries.

Meanwhile the main occupation force was assembled in Bombay. It numbered fewer than seven hundred officers and men, about half of them Indian sepoys. The arsenal included one hundred thousand musket balls and one thousand nine hundred shells for twelve-pounder howitzers. Chests containing 8000 dollars (about £1600) were reckoned sufficient for the first three months of the expedition's expenses. Two ships of the Royal Navy, HMS *Volage* and HMS *Cruizer*, transported the force to Aden where they joined Haines in Front Bay on 18 January 1839.

The formidable harbour fortress of Sira Island, whose batteries had punished the Portuguese severely in their unsuccessful attempt to capture Aden three centuries before, was bombarded from two sides at 10 a.m. on 19 January. The shore batteries were badly handled, and fell to an assault from the beach. Ninety minutes after the first shot was fired troops were landed on the beach in front of the town. They met little resistance. The inhabitants were crowded into the Aidrus Mosque under a white flag, and the entire Crater area was quickly occupied. Two Britons had been killed and three wounded. Arab casualties, mainly from the bombardment, were over one hundred.

An order went out to disarm prisoners and set them free outside the British defensive perimeter. A group of prisoners killed a sergeant and an interpreter who tried to take away their daggers, probably not understanding that they were to be freed and not slaughtered. Twelve prisoners were shot in the ensuing mêlée and British casualties for the day rose to four killed, eleven wounded.

The Arab defenders, estimated at one thousand rifles, left behind thirty-three heavy guns together with three thousand pounds of powder and twelve hundred cannon balls. Agents of rival powers had clearly given rather more than verbal encouragement for resistance to a British settlement.

The Union Jack was raised for the first time in Aden – over the seaside palace of the Sultan of Lahej, though the building was to stay in the ownership of the Lahej ruling family throughout British control of Aden. At that time it was one of the few buildings suitable for occupation. Little remained of the forgotten Golden Age of a thousand years before except water tanks choked with the silt and rubble of centuries of neglect, crumbled walls marking once-extensive water catchment channels. All that remained of the Salamah Mosque, built in the early eighth century, was a tall minaret. Haines was deeply impressed with one relic of the past, a road with each block of stone individually fitted, that ran along the ridge near the summit of Mount Shamshan, still much as Haines saw it when the British pulled out 129 years later.

The mixed population of about 250 Jews, 50 Indians, and 300

Arabs and Somalis lived in some ninety tumbledown houses and in shelters of reed matting. The Indians, known as Banians, controlled such trade as there was. The Somalis ran cattle dhows from Berbera returning with rice, tobacco and blue cloth. The Jews were artisans, making earrings and other ornaments for the tribal aristocracy of the hinterland.

The Jews were also the porters and bricklayers, and had, hitherto, hired themselves out in more prosperous Lahej. Henceforth they were to find plenty of work in Aden. Troops were also put to work repairing and extending the crumbling walls and watch-towers of the ancient defences and building barracks and houses.

Sultan Mahsin tarried hardly any time before sending emissaries to sign a document of submission, fearing that Haines might use the excuse of battle to bite off more territory, perhaps even the lush river oasis where he made his capital. He blamed his sons and asked, 'Forgive me and give me my pension'. Haines made arrangements for the first annual payment under the terms previously agreed for the commercial purchase of Aden as a property. This was generous since Britain was in Aden by right of conquest, a right then generally acknowledged, and widely pertaining in the world today, even in Europe.

Haines, by this time, was adept at dealing with Arabs, and he quickly developed an efficient intelligence service in neighbouring tribal capitals. Thus he was aware of plots to storm Aden and throw the British into the sea. The rulers of Lahej and Fadhli states put aside old enmities and met for the first time in their lives at Nobeir Maidee fort near Sheik Othman to plot a combined assault.

The defenders were ready when four thousand Bedouin attacked on 11 November. The tribesmen came under devastating fire from their rear, directed from boats in Back Bay, as they stormed Main Pass. They suffered more than two hundred dead, including twenty-four sheiks. This was due to the disciplined steadiness of the defenders, not superior fire power. The British percussion rifles gave only slightly more rapid fire capability than the tribesmen's flint-locks.

Two more attacks came in 1840. The first was in May when a tented camp was looted in a temporary break-through, and the property displayed in Lahej as proof of victory; the second in July when three hundred Arabs fell in murderous crossfire from boats offshore. An attack on the pro-British Sultan of tiny Bir Ahmed (present day Little Aden) was also beaten off.

Haines was convinced after this that persuasive argument had no more than temporary effect on the Arab mind. Taxed with breaking a promise an Arab notable told him blandly, 'It is our custom'. He was advocating a punitive expedition to Lahej to counter Arab taunts that the British were only brave behind stone walls. He saw such an expedition as the only way to achieve peace based on respect for British power. He wrote to Bombay, 'I have visited nearly every part of Arabia and the tribes in the neighbourhood of Aden are more treacherous and false than any other. Justice and right thinking is unknown to them. They are a people incapable of estimating the value of good government'.

But his masters in India, recently mortified by a disastrous punitive expedition to Kabul, were against any British involvement outside Aden. For this reason Haines's earlier requests for cavalry had been refused. His proposal to march on Lahej was vetoed with the tart comment, 'If Aden cannot be made a valuable acquisition without entering into aggressive warfare with the Arab chiefs of the interior, the sooner the place is abandoned the better'. In the wake of the loss of the American colonies many more people in Britain were casting doubt on the morality of Britannia's realm reaching 'wider still and wider'.

Eventually Haines was authorized to show the flag and its potential power by an expedition as far as Sheik Othman, eight miles outside the earliest British perimeter, along the road to Lahej town. The marching column, lacking cavalry, was at a disadvantage against harassment from Arabs on horses and camels. But disciplined and accurate shooting caused many casualties to the mounted Arabs. The column paused at Nobeir Maidee to blow up the fort where the Arab leaders had met to plan attacks on Aden, and bivouacked through the midday heat at Sheik Othman. They marched back to Aden in the cool of evening. British casualties were four wounded and one death from heat-stroke.

Meanwhile carpenters, blacksmiths and builders were recruited in Bombay and elsewhere, and a decision was made on the siting of a permanent cantonment. The isolated headland of Ras Tarshyne, beyond the ridges of Jebel Shamshan from Crater's old town and harbour, was strongly favoured for scenic beauty and cool breezes from the open ocean. But lack of water and the distance around the encircling rock walls from Crater made it impracticable at that time. The Crater area was so much easier to defend. Barracks and houses were built along the shoreline of Front Bay. Beyond a road named the Esplanade from that time, a new town was laid out with sections each for Arab, Indian and Jewish citizens. Along Front Bay there are still houses that might have been transported from Victorian India, high-ceiling bungalows with broad verandas, huge windows and flat roofs solidly built of local stone, the only building material available at that time. Most timber and iron was imported from Bombay, building workers came from Mocha, the Yemen coffee port on the Red Sea. Bakers and cooks were also imported from Mocha.

The rain catchment walls were repaired, watchtowers and gun emplacements rebuilt, and huge coal stockpiles accumulated.

Soon Aden was the main port for an increasing volume of goods to the sheikdoms of the hinterland and the isolated agricultural valleys of the Yemen beyond mountains rising out of the desert sixty miles inland.

Throughout these pioneer years the Egyptian-backed Sherif of Mocha, the tiny Red Sea port through which all of Yemen's rich coffee crop passed, was a tireless intriguer against a British settlement in Aden. At the beginning of the nineteenth century American ships were loading some 9000 bales of Yemen's total exports of 13,000 bales, pushing up the price sharply. Under Mohamed Ali's occupation the American traders were being charged only half the seven-and-a-half per cent duty charged to British traders.

Just the same American ships began switching to Aden when the British secured the port there and trade deals might be completed with more assurance. It was also closer than Mocha to the coffee-growing areas of Yemen. The Sherif of Mocha lowered his duties further still to attract American ships back.

Haines then showed a touch of commercial genius. In 1848 Aden ceased to charge any duty at all on any goods transiting or sold in its markets. So began its fame as an emporium for duty-free bargains. Within five years Aden was the main port for Yemen and Mocha became a ghost town as four thousand of its inhabitants moved to Aden. Four thousand camels, each carrying three hundred pounds of coffee, were arriving in Aden each year, a sideline that brought vast new wealth to the coaling depot's treasury.

The American trade alone was worth about £50,000. Ships

from Boston brought cotton goods for sale in the interior and sailed home with coffee and hides. Already these ocean-going ships could refit in Aden. It was, by the middle of the century, little more than a decade from Haines's landing, a boom town of 20,000 inhabitants, with an annual trade of £600,000. It was more than a military post defending a coaling station, and the Government of Bombay decreed in 1853 that 'consideration must be given to the people of Aden as well as for the preservation of the proper efficacy of the garrison'.

The military lobby reacted to this threat to the supremacy of its interests in the new imperial fortress. A military committee discovered that Haines had been careless with the treasury, neglecting to carry out routine monthly tallies of the reserves from the beginning of the settlement's history thirteen years before. The coin, in various currencies, had been kept in boxes and moved through a succession of lock-ups in the care of officials and clerks. It was laboriously counted and a deficiency of £28,198 was discovered in a total expenditure of £1,250,000 over the period. Haines, whose salary as political agent in Aden was £2400 a year, shrugged it off with an impatient explanation (echoing sentiments of men of action against mere accountants down the ages), 'There were more important things to do in Aden than count money'.

So the man who founded the Aden that was to be destroyed by the voracious cannibalism of Arab politics in the late sixties of this century, was dismissed, recalled to Bombay, and put on trial for embezzlement. He was acquitted by a jury, tried again on different charges and acquitted a second time. Then company officials, envious of his achievements, fearful his presence in London might win him through to the recognition he so clearly deserved, committed him to a debtors' prison for the balance of the deficiency in the treasury that still remained after his Aden property was forcibly sold in his absence. His wife and son awaited him in their Sussex home through six years he served in a debtors' prison. He died of dysentery at the age of fifty-eight aboard ship in Bombay harbour, on his way home at last. His body was taken ashore and buried in Colaba cemetery under a stone that bears only his name and the date of his death. There was no other memorial. A century later the head of an Indian merchant family in Aden was faithfully arranging for a bouquet on the grave in distant Bombay each year on the anniversary of his death.

His achievements as the founder of the great entrepot port

were never properly recognized. Few of tens of thousands of Europeans who have served in Aden ever heard of him. But when the last of them were evacuated in 1967 Arabs still commonly referred to the British as 'the children of Haines'.

2 Duty-Free Emporium

Haines's masterstroke of free trade through Aden assured its prosperity, acting as an incentive to traders to set up shop and make the port a magnet for ships of all nations. Only its distance from the direct Far East shipping routes around the Cape limited its booming growth. That was soon to be changed. Already a French consul in Egypt named Ferdinand de Lesseps had gained Mohamed Ali's interest for his dream of a ship canal cutting the sand dunes between Suez and the Mediterranean. Its opening in 1869 made Aden a port of call for every ship sailing between Europe and the Far East by this new shorter sea route. Aden's prosperity bounded, its population multiplied, its strategic importance immensely increased. The tiny harbour on the Crater side was supplanted by new jetties, piers and dock installations outside the natural defences of the rock walls with their rebuilt fortifications. On the other side of the Aden peninsula a new area known as Steamer Point became the new centre of British life. Mansions for the colonial Raj crowned the spurs above near-by Tarshyne beach.

A lighthouse and subsidiary bunkering facilities were established on Perim Island, scene of the earliest 'secret' British military establishment in Arabia, attracting settlement from the near-by Yemen mainland to an erstwhile waterless island in the Strait of Bab al-Mandeb, commanding the narrow entrance to the Red Sea.

By 1940 Aden was surpassed only by London and Liverpool for tonnage of shipping handled among all the ports of the Commonwealth. Along with all the other vast territories of the East India Company, Aden was transferred from company ownership to the crown following the Indian Mutiny of 1857.

The sheikdoms and emirates of the hinterland were left to get on with their traditional feuding until a start was made in bringing them into treaty relationship with Britain in 1858. The first Treaty of Protection giving Britain charge of external defence and foreign affairs was signed that year by the Sultan of Lahej. It was followed by twenty-one similar treaties over the next fifty years and the tribal 'badlands' of the hinterland became known as the Aden Protectorates.

Its borders edged on Saudi Arabia and the Dhofar region of Oman, empty desert areas, in the east; but most of its frontiers were with Yemen, a land firmly closed to alien infidels, barely seventy miles from Aden at its nearest point, but centuries away in terms of social and political change.

Few people from Aden ventured into the wild desert and mountain land of the Protectorate covering 112,000 square miles around the 75 square miles of the British colony. Most of the 300,000 population was in the fertile Hadramaut far to the east of Aden. Inland from Aden, beyond the lush oasis of near-by Lahej, the desert ended in a huge massif rising to 6000 feet, a huge natural barrier, closing the way to Yemen to all but the hardiest travellers, thirty miles and more before they could reach a political line on the map supposedly marking the frontier. The harsh terrain bred a hungry, isolated, savage people, living in fortified villages, their ideas dominated by rifles and daggers always at hand to guard hard-worked terraced fields and flocks from covetous neighbours. Sentinels manned rocky watchtowers ready to shoot approaching strangers on sight. Blood feuds were fought generations after the original quarrel was forgotten. Populations were counted by the number of armed men and boys.

Into this land Britain sent political agents to protect the rulers from the intrigues of rival powers. They were that special breed of men for whom the old empire might have been invented, gifted intellectuals with an almost monkish bent, spellbound by the desert's poetry as well as its harsh challenge, content with living in an all-male society. Most were natural linguists from the Indian Army or civil service in the Indian Empire or the Sudan.

In the beginning they were usually scholars of Urdu, the camp language of Moghul India, written in sanscrit symbols in which the languages of Arabic and Persian tongues are also inscribed. Mostly they were romantics, lured by nostalgia over the writings of Richard Burton, Lawrence; sometimes by the Bedouin Arab's tolerance of homosexuality in a world then rudely intolerant of sexual deviation.

Skilfully these lone representatives of the distant power kept tribal feuding within acceptable limits, sowed seeds of more enlightened rule, and with such slender resources as were available in an area that came low down the list for imperial benefices, used their intimacies with the sheiks to initiate primitive schools, clinics, improved agriculture and transport. It was not until after World War Two that a series of supplementary advisory treaties reinforced these tricky relationships with some kind of control over an increased trickle of financial and technical aid.

By the eve of World War One the current incumbent in power in Lahej, addressed by this time as 'His Highness, Sir Ahmed Fadhl, Sultan of Lahej', wrote to the British Resident, as the senior British official was called, in these terms:

'Time has passed and ill feeling has given place to affection towards you. Aden in your hands is as if it were still in mine. Aden has become an important fortress in your hands, the centre of trade and the port is rich. We rejoice at its progress.'

During the second year of World War One Turkish forces crossed the border from Yemen and occupied Dhala, seat of a border sultan. They advanced along the busy trade route to Aden until their march was halted at the colony's first defence lines beyond Sheik Othman, close to what was the race-course before it became Khormaksar airport.

Aden businessmen enlisted in a colonial militia to help contingents of the Indian Army man the trenches opposite the unspirited Turkish siege lines. The enemy camp at the gates ended weekend picnics in the desert but caused little serious inconvenience.

Arabs were enlisted as soldiers for the first time. An infantry battalion, with headquarters at Sheik Othman, furnished garrisons for Perim and the Kamaran Islands some three hundred miles inside the Red Sea. In 1926 the Perim garrison mutinied, murdered its British commander and fled with the garrison treasury to near-by Yemen.

The RAF was made responsible for Aden's protection in 1928. Air surveillance with its threat of punitive bombing – the flying gunboats of the overlapping colonial and air ages – were a swift, easy answer to control of the tribes. RAF uniforms were worn by the Aden Protectorate Levies, which included a camel troop. In 1939 an anti-aircraft wing was added, and it succeeded in shooting down an enemy bomber during an Italian raid from their African colony of Somaliland. The Levies later supervised the training of Tribal Guards, a ragbob militia equipped with rifles supplied as annual rewards to tribal chiefs believed to be loyal to British suzerainty.

A by-product of the 1918 defeat and extinction of the Ottoman Empire was the emergence of a more troublesome neighbour in the Yemen. The Imam Yahya's dynasty stretched back to the ninth century, claiming descent from the Prophet Mohamed through Hassan, son of Mohamed's daughter, Fatima. Thus he was the chief priest of the Zeidis, clergy of a Shia minority sect that ruled Yemen. He kept his realm in a state of medieval backwardness, maintaining tribal loyalties by an ancient Yemen custom of holding the sons of his sheiks for schooling as boarders in his royal palace. He shunned foreign intercourse, and kept diplomatic contacts to a minimum. Yemen was almost as isolated and closed to the curious as the Forbidden Land of Tibet.

His ambitions to restore his power throughout the territory of the Yemen-based empires of the ancient world brought him rapidly into war with the new Arabian power of Saudi Arabia, ending in defeat and the loss of Yemen's northern regions of Asir and Najran.

Although Yemen had lost control of the Southern Arabian tribes a hundred years before Haines founded Aden, Imam Yahya claimed the whole of the south including the British colony. He refused to recognize a border demarcation treaty between Britain and the former Turkish rulers of Yemen. Frequent raids and incursions by Yemen tribesmen were contained by RAF bombing and strafing for fifteen years until the Imam was constrained to sign a treaty recognizing the status quo.

This was signed at Sanaa, one of twin Yemen capitals, in 1934, and was to last for an initial forty years. Yemen caused little trouble after that even during the lowest ebb of British fortunes in the Second World War. Italian blandishments failed to incite new frontier incursions.

Italian planes bombed Aden and Perim Island during World War Two but otherwise it was an oasis of peace remote from huge battles far to the east and west. Its role was as a key refuelling and resupply port for ships plying east and west through Suez. Some loss of revenue caused by the diversion of shipping around the Cape, avoiding more perilous transit of the Mediterranean, was a precursor of more serious closures to come.

As World War Two ended Yemen's Crown Prince Ahmed began to stir fresh tribal unrest from Taiz, closest major town to Aden, where he was governor. About the same time a Free Yemen Party, hostile to the despotic Imam, was active among Aden's huge floating population of Yemeni workers.

Frontier tensions increased after the assassination of the octogenarian Imam Yahya and the accession of Ahmed to the Imamate in 1948. The Aden question came up at the United Nations for the first time in an uproar over an RAF strike against a fort built by Ahmed's army inside the protected state of Beihan in 1949. Yemen, admitted to the UN only two years earlier, used the incident to renew the old territorial claim. Doubtless it was inspired by rumours of an oil strike in the frontier region of Shabwah where an oil exploration company had recently made a survey with negative results. Britain used the new Imam's resort to international channels as a lever to open diplomatic relations and a British mission was established in Taiz under a chargé d'affaires.

The Imam also complained that a new British forward policy in the protectorates was contrary to the treaty guaranteeing the status quo. The Imam was convinced that the British interest was aroused by knowledge of the existence of oil. The truth was that the current governor of Aden, Sir Tom Hickenbotham, was appalled at the old policy of minimum involvement in the protectorate, making the hinterland a museum-piece preserve of Arabia *antiqua*. The existing treaties of protection were designed to hold the Turks and the Yemenis at a distance, and no more.

The more developed states of Quaiti and Kathiri in the distant Eastern group of protectorates had asked for British administrative assistance in the late thirties, and advisory treaties had been drawn up to cover a closer British involvement. Under these the rulers undertook to accept the advice of a British resident political officer on all matters except those concerning Muslim custom and religion. Over the following decade several minor states followed suit.

Governer Hickenbotham opened a political offensive to bring the remaining states into this closer involvement and began energizing reform in the states already in this little exploited advisory relationship. He was faced with resentment from the rulers who were jealous of their despotic rights. Some had entered into treaties believing this would give them greater authority by bringing British military muscle to their support in dealings with wayward villages. Instead they found that stubborn refusal to institute reform could mean their replacement by more agreeable tribal successors. The advisory treaty was generally regarded as a cloak for British rule.

One of those refusing to sign an Advisory Treaty was the Sultan of Lahej, ruler of the area closest to Aden and straddling the busy trade road to Yemen. Sultan Fadhl modelled himself on Egypt's King Farouk who had abrogated the Anglo-Egyptian Treaty, ended the Anglo-Egyptian condominium in the Sudan, and actively encouraged terrorist gangs to attack British soldiers in the Suez Canal Zone. He also aped Farouk's notorious depravities. In 1952 he ordered the execution of three cousins in his presence after accusing them of plotting against him. When word of this reached Government House, twenty-four miles away in Aden, Governor Hickenbotham sent a terse invitation to Sultan Fadhl to call on him. The Sultan ignored the summons and the Protectorate Levies were ordered into Lahej to 'restore order'. Sultan Fadhl fled to Yemen and induced the Imam to protest to Britain at the interference in the internal affairs of Lahej. A political agent named Kennedy Trevaskis (later to become Aden's governor and target of the first terrorist hand grenade) was told by a crowd in the market place that the people wanted the benevolent rule of the British. They wanted Lahej to be taken over as a colony like Aden.

The next Lahej ruler, Sultan Ali, younger brother of the decamped despot, was suave, intelligent, westernized and believed British guidance was necessary to modernize his state. He accepted an advisory treaty, and the forward policy was given fresh boost.

Towards the end of 1952 Mr Kennedy Trevaskis, Adviser for the Western Protectorate, put forward a plan for a federation of the hinterland states. Governor Hickenbotham, thinking along similar lines, worked with him on drawing up a blueprint. It was backed by London and put to the rulers at a conference in January 1954. It envisaged separate federations initially for the western and eastern groups of protectorates because of greater administrative development in those eastern states that had benefited from advisory treaties signed twelve and more years earlier. Federal responsibilities were to cover customs, communications, education and public health. Internal authority in member states was to continue in the hands of the traditional ruler. The whole idea was angrily rejected by the rulers.

This move towards nationhood for the southern tribes of Arabia was violently denounced as a British ploy to extend colonialism throughout the area. In Yemen the Imam feared the establishment of an independent state, dominated by Shafai Muslims, on his southern borders. Two of every three of his own subjects were Shafai. The Shafai regarded the Yemen's ruling minority sect, the Zeidi, with the kind of hostility that the Catholic Irish have for William of Orange.

The Arab League, a loose association of Arab states originally founded by the British, viewed the Zeidi Imamate in Yemen with little satisfaction, but they publicly backed the Imam. They denounced the move for federation in Southern Arabia as a British imperialistic ploy to divide the Arab world by the creation of a new pro-western nationalism.

In Egypt, meanwhile, a coup by a group of young officers caught the imagination of youth throughout the Arab world. They saw Gamal Abdul Nasser, the emergent leader of a new dynamic Egypt, as a second Mohamed Ali. He would end the habit of Arab submission to foreigners, remove the shame of defeat at the hands of Jewish settlers, right the Arab wrongs in Palestine.

Nasser returned to Cairo from a euphoric Afro-Asian Conference at Bandoeng in 1955 and declared a cold war on Britain. He was soon to hot it up. Cairo's Voice of the Arabs radio blew up skirmishing, instigated by the Imam from across the Yemen border, into a major war in which 'colonialism was in full retreat from the Arab homeland'.

But no ripple of these desert clashes disturbed the bustling commerce of Aden's duty-free bazaars, crowded with bargain hunters from every passing liner. Aden was enjoying a fresh surge in prosperity. This one stemmed from a decision to build an oil refinery to replace the British Petroleum refinery at Abadan nationalized by the demagogic Persian nationalist Mohamed Mossadegh. Prime Minister Clement Attlee's appeal to the International Court against this arbitrary action was ineffective. Till then an automatic response to such a challenge would have been the deployment of an Indian Army division.

The new refinery created an atmosphere of gold rush. The opening of new job opportunities for unskilled labourers brought a huge new influx of workers from Yemen. The site was twenty-five miles by road around the bay from Aden town, two miles of salt water directly across from Steamer Point. It was named Little Aden. The colony's population, then touching 100,000, increased rapidly. A rash of new building was untidy, noisy, but for the most part outside the orbit of the British residents of Steamer Point.

For them Aden remained a microcosm of the British Indian Empire that had already disappeared into history. The tiny elite of Aden's 'little Raj' continued to enjoy the privileges of a master race.

The climate might be abominable, but they were still sahibs, their wives and daughters memsahibs. The Christmas pantomime, the New Year fancy dress party at the club, the Aden Levies Officers' Ball, the time-honoured diversions of annual occasions like these marked the passage of time between annual home leave in a tiny tropical community where the passing seasons merged into unchanging, muggy heat.

3 Potshot War

Nasser's campaign against the British in Aden began weeks after his prestigious 'victory' in the Suez War of 1956. The withdrawal of the British at Port Said, supposedly at the behest of the United Nations, was a clear pointer to immense possibilities elsewhere. The prejudices of delegates to the international forum were developing into an ultimate weapon in the armouries of leaders of what had then become known as the uncommitted world, practitioners of the crudest political opportunism, knowing how far the West was likely to lean over backwards not to offend them, believing they knew how far it was safe to play the blandishments of Moscow and Peking.

In the beginning a new colonial war in South Arabia went almost unnoticed in the old imperial capital. London was absorbed with agonizing inquests over Suez and Hungary, where the double standards of one rule of conduct expected of the capitalist west and anything goes for the communist eastern bloc were laid down as guidelines for decades ahead.

Cairo's Voice of the Arabs radio nightly singed the cool desert air with virulent allegations of continuing British aggression

L.S.–C

against the Arab homeland. Now the imperialist bully's victim was tiny, defenceless Yemen, a remote, almost unknown kingdom whose despotic rulers had hitherto shunned all contact with the changing world around them.

The desert and granite frontier between Yemen, surrounded by almost impenetrable mountains, and the protectorates had always been vaguely defined. Tribal disputes flared often across the frontier, over grazing in wadis where flash floods provided brief pasture every other year or so. Potshots from neighbours were a normal hazard of travel beyond village boundaries. It added zest to the hard life of survival in an environment cursed by nature, and amused the young scholars of Arab culture representing the Imperial power, the British officials who lived among them as honoured guests of their chief.

The Aden Protectorate Levies was trying to be umpire and keep the war games within sporting limits. Its officers and NCOs were seconded from the RAF regiment. Bedouin Arabs were recruited to fill the ranks. For the young Britons, some serving two years' compulsory national service, it was Kipling-style adventure in the tradition of the North-West Frontier of India. Occasionally they clashed with raiding tribesmen from Yemen armed with ancient Turkish rifles and barbarous-looking curved swords and daggers. For two decades, since the last highly effective demonstration of old style power politics by an RAF bombing raid on the twin Yemen capital of Taiz, regular patrols to show the imperial flag had been sufficient to maintain a status quo.

Odd skirmishes lent flavour to the languor of cocktail parties in Aden, safe behind its desert moat, where in an area smaller than Rutland, then England's smallest county, a polyglot population lived in well-regulated peace. But in 1953 British prestige suffered a humiliating reverse. The Levies were driven from the field in an operation to subdue the Rabizi tribe of the Wadi Hatib which was taking regular subsidies from the Imam. A fort established in the market place at Robat was abandoned and blown up by triumphant tribesmen. The Levies, armed with .303 rifles and sten guns, trained for ceremonial parades, were clearly outmatched by the sturdy hill fighters. Word of the defeat rang around the mountains, echoed through the Arab world, but was hardly noticed at all in Britain, busy then with the Queen's coronation, the conquest at last of Everest and a double murder on Teddington towpath. It did, however, cause some searching reappraisal in Aden. The Levies were taken over by the old War Office, its officers were taught Arabic and desert war tactics, and tribal fighters were recruited to its ranks. From that time strongholds were sited close by accessible landing strips.

At the beginning of 1957 a serious military threat developed on the frontier. In place of old Turkish rifles tribesmen were using modern rifles and machine-guns made in Czechoslovakia.

On the last day of 1956 – watershed year in the Arab love-hate relationship with Britain – a major incursion into the Aden protectorate developed from the Yemen frontier town of Quataba. Raiding parties were clearly under professional military direction, and more and more tribes were joining the insurgents.

Such was still the potshot nature of the fighting that the only reported casualty that first day was an Arab girl of eight, killed by a ricochet. She was the first of many hundreds of innocent Arab bystanders to be killed or mutilated in the indiscriminate urban guerrilla warfare that was to come later in Aden itself.

The fighting escalated as the Levies intervened. Large numbers of raiders ravaged the area, burning precious crops, looting and carrying off women and livestock. A political adviser, Ernest Kennedy, narrowly escaped when his car was ambushed and the RAF was called in to strafe the invaders. This stirred some passing interest in Britain, and a howl of protest in the corridors and debating chambers of the United Nations. The priest-king of Yemen, who called himself 'The Sword of Islam', called for volunteers from the Arab lands and Russia to stem a new British aggression.

I arrived in Aden as troop reinforcements were being airlifted from Kenya, then the main British military base East of Suez. Within hours of landing at the international airport I took off from the same runway in an RAF Pembroke, a twin engine transport plane, that served as an express link between the Aden base and the war front.

We flew for an hour over a white glare of sand and livid rock, pitching and bucking amid funnels of searing air. Jolting a few feet above jagged peaks we came to the town of Dhala, a huddle of multi-storey fortified houses crowning a hillock in the middle of a narrow plateau. Eight miles away beyond the frontier the white painted town of Quataba, launching pad of the invasion, glinted in the sun. The plane banked at a crazy angle with rock faces rising sheer from the edge of the plateau so close that crevasses loomed a few feet beyond the wing tips. Moments later we bounced along loose, broken rock chips of an air strip.

A dust cloud indicated a vehicle approaching fast. A ten-ton lorry lurched to a stop a few yards away as we jumped from the plane. From the lorry long-haired Arabs of the Aden Protectorate Levies raced Indian file towards near-by hillocks, rifles trailing. Behind came another lorry with more soldiers. Then three armoured cars crashed through the scrub fanning out around the plane. Last came a Land-Rover to carry our small press party to the Levies camp. We drove along a rough track. Girls, faces painted yellow, models of beauty in those harsh parts, peeped at us as we passed fortified houses.

The Levies camp was surrounded by an eight-foot stone wall, surmounted by rocky watchtowers with loopholes for rifles. Within the outer wall, stone screens sheltered sleeping tents, the cookhouse and vehicle parks lined paths.

The craggy peaks around looked deserted, but at night tribesmen lay among them taking potshots into the camp. An officer explained, 'The shooting is more noisy than dangerous'. All the same the Levies and the RAF armoured car crews lived a life of siege on that hot 4500-foot plateau among the towering crags. Once every three weeks a road convoy took two days to cover the road from Aden, under fire for half the journey by tribesmen penetrating fifty miles inside British territory. Two Pembroke flights a week brought them fresh provisions and mail. Beer, piping hot in cans, was strictly rationed. So were cigarettes. The commanding officer had seen his wife and two young sons for only three days since they had arrived in Aden from their home in Kingston, Surrey, six months earlier. There was just no room in the planes for leave-taking. Extra flights were laid on only for frequent dysentery cases.

In the previous two weeks the RAF had flown more than sixty sorties against tribesmen in blue paint, feathered headdresses and bandoliers. Among the mud-coloured crags they were almost immune from ground retaliation, so Venom fighters and slower Lincoln bombers were sent out to strafe the marauding bands. With plentiful cover in boulder-strewn wadis and among the crags the tribesmen escaped mostly with a bad fright.

The British airmen carried out these punitive attacks under strict orders to stay on the protectorate side of the frontier, but Sanaa Radio and Cairo's Voice of the Arabs broadcasts denounced them as attacks inside Yemen. Yemen complaints about bombing of its towns by the RAF were accepted with sympathy throughout Afro-Asia. Agents backed the broadcasts with drawings of Egyptian soldiers shooting at British bombers. This propaganda was much more dangerous than the bullets. British operations were frequently hamstrung because every counter move required high-level permission from officials looking over their shoulders at likely interpretations made in the debating chambers of the UN. Little wonder that the rulers of the protectorate states were seriously worrying even then that Britain might leave them to fall under Yemen annexation in the end.

The ruler of beleaguered Dhala, the Emir Shaaful bin Ali bin Shaif, was badly frightened. I met him in a sandbagged house which was home and office of his British adviser, a place destined to make headlines a year later when the next British adviser was besieged for several days there. The Emir toyed with a gold and ivory handled dagger, wickedly curved, stuck into the folds of a silk cummerbund. Through an interpreter he told me, 'The situation gets worse every day. I blame the British. Under their treaty they are supposed to protect my people. But they do not send enough troops.'

As we talked one hundred Government Guards in black turbans manned sandbagged strongpoints, eyes and rifles trained on the surrounding crags.

The Emir, spindle legged like his poor, ragged subjects who scraped a sparse living among sand and rock, was dressed in comic opera garb. He wore a green blazer, wine-coloured pullover, blue shirt, multi-coloured turban, brown shoes and patterned ankle-length socks – a tribute to the wardrobes and generosity of a succession of British advisers.

When he left to return to his mud-fortress palace he rode a fine chestnut Arab stallion with his nondescript bodyguard sprinting along around him, one wearing a WAAF officer's jacket. His adviser, Mr Robin Young, then aged thirty, was a man with a price on his head, living a rugged and lonely life. He said he liked Arabs, delighted in their language, liked their food, admired their finer qualities.

Back in Aden colonial life seemed even more unreal. At the roof restaurant in the Rock hotel a four-piece band made offbeat music. It was too hot even for the colonial Englishman to wear a jacket. Instead he compromised with a cummerbund to match his black tie. In the fetid heat only the very young had energy to dance. No breeze stirred the palms around the harbour, busy once more after the doldrums of the temporary closure of Suez.

Around the edge of the roof nawabs of commerce sat long over cigars, talking between frequent swallows from tumblers of Scotch, with colonial officials and military men. They gossiped of ships, cargoes, tennis tournaments, polo and county cricket far away in England. Wives generally sat apart talking of the newest arrival from home, the latest romantic attachments, and the ever-present problem of servants. There was little talk and less worry about the war which young Britons were fighting only ninety miles away across the desert. That blinding glare of sand and rock by day and painter's dream by moonlight, was like a solidified extension of the ocean. Their Aden was an island.

I was invited to the white-colonnaded Government House to meet the Governor, Sir William Luce. We sipped cocktails in bougainvillea and hibiscus-scented gardens overlooking the wide bay. The Governor, also Commander-in-Chief, talked of the capital the United Nations debating society made of every military measure he took.

News came that a force of five hundred Yemen irregulars had captured the town of Hadeya, ten miles inside the Protectorate, after a pitched battle with loyal tribesmen. I flew to the area in an airlift of troops of the Durham Light Infantry. We landed at a sandy strip near the town of Beihan, 180 miles by air from Aden. Planes with troops and ammunition shuttled there all day, and Brigadier Rankin, the one-legged army chief, arrived by helicopter to supervise operations.

On the frontier at Manawa, just over a rocky escarpment from the airstrip, British troops had just fought their first pitched battle of the frontier troubles. It had gone on from dawn to dusk the previous day. A force estimated at five hundred strong, some dressed in the green denim uniform of the Yemen regular army, crossed a four-hundred-yard belt of flat sand between the frontier and a steeply rising crag. Under cover of darkness they had dug a trench across the flat sand of the gully to hold up vehicles. The normal dawn patrol of RAF armoured cars was caught in a heavy crossfire and forced to turn back. The fire was heavier from the Yemen side of the frontier than from the crags on the protectorate side. That night the intruders withdrew under cover of darkness back to the safety of Yemen.

From the air I saw a well, fortified by gun positions, just inside the Yemen border as recognized by Britain. In that parched landscape it had been used by villagers from both sides of the frontier until the Yemenis denied it to the people of what they termed 'enemy occupied South Yemen'.

The local chief, black-bearded Sherif Hussein, was cheered by this firm defeat of invaders. He ordered a black goat and three chickens to be slaughtered for lunch.

His mud-built fortified palace was guarded by about twenty riflemen. As he led us on a tour of the town a ragged bodyguard of riflemen, stiff with bandoliers and daggers, escorted him. While lunch was being slaughtered at the back of the house we sat in his shanty office talking through an interpreter. On the wall was a picture of the Queen, and near by was his certificate of the Order of the British Empire, hanging in a frame. The Sherif, slim and tall, was a fine figure with his beard and burning, deepset black eyes, dressed in a splendid turban and colourful robes. He fingered a jewelled revolver in a pearl embroidered holster strapped across his waist to balance a huge curved dagger also heavily jewelled.

He said, 'People across the frontier think I am a tail of the British, and they will not leave me alone until I cease to have friendship with the British.' He looked at a picture of the Queen; 'The Great Queen is Defender of the Faith. I have told these people who insult me and try to make me break my treaty with the British that the British help us, but do not rule us. I cannot have my lands at the mercy of Yemen robbers, but I am not strong enough to stay independent without foreign help. I cannot have the help of communists because they are against religion. I cannot have the help of Egyptians or Saudis because they would want to rule me as well.'

He added, 'The man behind the trouble is Jemal' – Gamal Abdul Nasser of Egypt.

We climbed narrow mud stairs to an upper room where a slave poured water over our hands, and a second slave held out a towel. We sat cross-legged on carpet with a feast spread before us on a scarlet cloth. There was not a piece of cutlery in sight. We ate with our right hands – the left being regarded in Arabia as the unclean hand reserved for toilet purposes. The goat we had seen driven into the courtyard earlier was deliciously spiced, though somewhat underdone and difficult to eat with one hand. The chickens were easier to deal with. With it were bowls of spicey vegetables and fruit drinks served in stem glasses still marked with the small gold and red label of the Birmingham manufacturer.

That night insurgents sneaked back from Yemen to occupy two peak-top forts commanding the desert road to Manawa. Next day the Durhams, relieving the battle-weary Levies, crawled through scrub under cover of low-level strafing by rocket-firing Venom fighters. The Durhams mortared the forts and charged with the bayonet. The insurgents retired behind the frontier and stayed there. The situation was under control once more. The potshot war spluttered on unnoticed till the next major flare-up.

4 Nasser's Fifth Column

Colonial Society was shattered when Nasser's intrigues moved suddenly right up to Aden's doorstep at the height of the social season of 1958. A well-liked cocktail party figure, Sir Ali Abdul Karim, installed as Sultan of the neighbouring Lahej state after British military intervention six years earlier, was himself deposed as British troops occupied his capital.

A month earlier the Imam of Yemen had taken his kingdom into the Nasser camp in a nominal association with the united regimes of Egypt and Syria called the United Arab States. This had inspired Sultan Ali, who had gradually become a firm Arab nationalist, to go one better. He planned the bold step of abrogating his protection and advisory treaties with Britain and taking Lahej into the United Arab Republic, a two-months'-old tight political union of Egypt and Syria destined to last only till 1961 when Egyptian troops and officials, having made themselves insufferable, were expelled from Syria.

Sultan Ali's plans became known to Government House in Aden, and British officials, long disappointed in their protégé sultan, decided to suffer his wavering loyalties no longer. He had 'overstepped the mark' as it was quaintly put in a public statement about his replacement by a more pliant relative, an elderly uncle.

The ambitious Sir Ali had committed himself to the earliest political movement in the protectorate states – the South Arabia League which aimed at an independent unitary South Arabia. It was opposed to union with Yemen though strongly influenced by

Nasser's Arab socialism in its earlier years. It had become clear to Sultan Ali that the British regarded him as too much of a playboy for him to have a lead role in plans for a federal state which he knew the British were determined to pursue. Instead he turned his dreams towards being an associate of Nasser as leader of a South Arabian Region of the United Arab Republic. Lahej was the only state in the protectorates to employ Egyptian teachers, one of Cairo's early major exports after the emergence of President Nasser. These stimulators of the Nasser myth among the Arab young outnumbered local teaching staff.

The ploy to regain full independence and present Britain with a *fait accompli* of union with Egypt was a clever try. Made five or six years later it might well have come off. But it came when Britain had no mind to forsake Aden, no thought to reduce status as a global power.

In the politics of ruthless violence soon to dominate the Aden scene the South Arabian League was anyway a non-starter. It was founded by three brothers named Jifri with a touching faith in achieving their aims by methods learned from British tutors. They went on pamphleteering, lobbying, giving press conferences almost to the end. Nobody took the League into serious account.

The deposed Sultan was exiled in Cairo, where two of the Jifri brothers had fled earlier after escaping a British attempt to arrest them for subversion. The third brother, the Lahej minister of education, was arrested and subsequently released. The commander of the Lahej state forces, another lion of the Aden salons, fled to Yemen with what is recorded only as 'a considerable number of men and some state funds'.

A decade later, known as plain Ali Abdul Kerim, the former Sultan was still haunting the Day and Night coffee bar in Cairo's Semiramis Hotel, like a ghost of promise passed. The struggle for trade union and mob power in Aden had long since made him irrelevant.

The disturbances in Lahej brought the other protectorate rulers to agreement with Government House in Aden that their only hope of future security was to combine in a federal state with a treaty providing for a British base in Aden.

The Aden colony itself – the only territory in the vast Arab world under complete British rule – was already the most politically advanced state in the Arabian Peninsula. Its cosmopolitan population (at 1955 census: 36,910 Aden Arabs, 18,991 protectorate

Arabs, 48,000 Yemenis, 15,817 Indians, 10,611 Somalis, 3763 Britons, 721 other Europeans, 831 Jews, and 2608 others, including Lebanese, Syrians and Americans) enjoyed reasonable prosperity despite the temporary closure of the Suez Canal on whose traffic it had grown and prospered over eight decades. The British base brought a basic £12 millions into the community chest, providing jobs for one-third of the work force. The new refinery at Little Aden made up for the period when bunkering went down by four-fifths. The business community had put on plenty of reserve fat, and the leaner months of the Suez closure brought no critical hardship.

Order reigned. No man or woman walked the street in fear. There was doubtless some resentment that the British enjoyed highest living standards, reserved the best beaches for themselves, remained aloof in their clubs, but any Adeni wearing a tie was able to dine and dance in hotel restaurants when a Briton without a tie was refused admission.

After ninety-eight years under the administration of the Indian Civil Service directed first from Bombay, later from Delhi, Aden had come directly under the Colonial Office as recently as 1937. This move was made largely under pressure from influential Indian citizens of Aden who feared incorporation in an independent India that was clearly soon to be a reality. Their feelings echoed the sentiments of a former Aden governor who had complained that the colony was treated by his superiors in India 'as if Aden was a small town in the Bombay Presidency'.

Another fourteen years passed before the Indian rupee ceased to be the colony's official currency, only to be replaced, presumably for minting convenience, by East African Shillings.

Despite its premier place in Arabian political development Aden's progress was slow by most British colonial standards. The first elections, held in December 1955, were for a mere four seats in a reconstituted Legislative Council of eighteen members which sat under the chairmanship of the governor. These four seats were newly set aside for elected representatives. Fourteen seats were reserved as before for officials and nominees of the governor. The elections were boycotted by a United Nationalist Front and the Aden Association, a conservative group of merchants, took three of the four elected seats.

Even these newly elected conservatives were dissatisfied with progress, and when Lord Lloyd, then Under-Secretary for the

Colonies, visited Aden in May 1956, eve of the Suez watershed in Anglo-Arab relations, the Aden Association put forward a package of moderate steps towards self-government. The main points were a legislature confined to elected members, an executive council drawn from its membership, Arabic as an official language with English, and a reduction in the number of British officials in senior administrative posts.

Lord Lloyd coldly rejected the petition, adding magisterially, 'The importance of Aden both strategically and economically within the Commonwealth is such that Her Majesty's Government cannot foresee the possibility of any fundamental relaxation of their responsibilities for the Colony'.

Just eighteen months later – little more than a year after the Suez débâcle – representative government took a long stride forward with a new constitution. This gave the Legislative Council twelve elected members, a majority of one over eleven officials and nominees although the Speaker was also appointed by the Governor. Three departmental posts also went to elected members, automatically giving them seats on the Governor's Executive Council. Arabic was also recognized as an alternative language to English in the Legislative Council.

Elections for the first three-year term of the new Legislative Council, held in January 1959, were this time boycotted by the Aden TUC, a fledgling organization flexing political muscle for the first time. The poll was only twenty-seven per cent. The Trade Union objection was mainly because the franchise was limited to British subjects or British-protected persons living in Aden who fulfilled minimum property or income qualifications. This reduced eligible voters to 21,554 in a population swollen to about 180,000. Indians, Pakistanis and Somalis could qualify as Commonwealth citizens. Few of the 60,000 Arabs from the protectorate met the financial qualifications. Some 70,000 other Arabs were Yemenis by nationality. These latter were the main rank and file membership of the trade unions.

To the short-sighted relief of colonial colonels and commercial nawabs the boycott excluded extreme nationalist leaders from the new legislature. Instead they turned to mob manipulation and agitation, and soon the Aden TUC emerged as the champion of Nasser-style Arab socialism.

Legal provision for trade unions was made in Aden in 1942, but it was 1953 before the first two Arab trade unions were registered. By 1956 when the Aden TUC was recognized by the International Confederation of Trade Unions, there were thirty affiliated unions with a membership of 22,000.

The International organization described the Aden TUC as the most highly developed trade union movement in the Middle East. From the start it was more interested in the political aims of Arab nationalism than in hours, holidays or pay. In 1959 more than eighty strikes cost 150,000 work days, damaging the everyday livelihood of the whole community, undermining efforts to attract international shipping business.

The colonial government called in a former trade unionist from Britain, a Mr Fellows, for consultation. On his advice an Industrial Relations Ordinance (forerunner of legislation that confounded a later British Labour government and later still brought down the Heath Conservative government) made strikes illegal by attempting to enforce arbitration.

On 15 August 1960, Aden TUC called a general strike. The port, airport, shops, restaurants were closed as the legislature passed the Bill by thirteen votes to eight. Some members had already left the chamber in protest.

Abdullah al-Asnag, Secretary-General of Aden TUC, emerged that day to enjoy a brief spell as the most powerful man in the colony. Most of his support was from the immigrant Yemen workers in the docks, the oil refinery and in building work.

Nasser's fifth column was well established.

5 Red Wolves of Radfan

Yemen's adherence to Egypt and Syria in March 1958 seemed likely to threaten Aden's security as never before. Instead it gave the colony a breathing space of almost seven years.

Imam Ahmed, ruler since the assassination of his father in 1948, reversed the traditional policy of total isolation, made contacts with Moscow and Peking, finally settled on Nasser to back him in a bid to push the tottering British imperialists into the Indian Ocean at Aden's Steamer Point. The winter campaign of 1957 had proved that his tribal fighters needed more sophisticated military support.

Instead his overtures to Nasser precipitated his own downfall. Egyptian advisers were not about to become tools of despotic empire building other than their own even in the battle against British imperialism. More important they knew that the Imam stood in the way of a Nasserite takeover of Aden. Few among the 80,000 Yemenis living in Aden would favour the Imam's cause.

The process of political education of chosen Yemen officers was slow and dangerous. The Imam was watchful. The Egyptian plotters were not ready to act until September 1962, shortly after Imam Ahmed's death. Then they fumbled the coup by failing to kill the new Imam Mohamed in an assault on his palace.

He escaped with wounds, and within weeks the new Yemen Republic had to be sustained by an Egyptian Expeditionary Force against royalist tribes who swarmed to the Imam's battle banners. Yemen began a bloody civil war that dragged on for more than a decade. Nasser's puppet government controlled the high plateau between the twin capitals, Taiz at the end of the lorry route from Aden, and Sanaa, a city under constant threat from royalist tribes in the flanking mountains. The cost in Egyptian blood, equipment and treasure has never been fully revealed, but it can fairly be said to have been on the scale of American losses in Vietnam. Not even Nasser's blanket censorship could cover up the flow of bereavements in so many Nile Delta villages or tales told by survivors, crippled farm boys and disillusioned young officers.

The enormous Egyptian military staff in Taiz soon found diversions from efforts to pin down elusive royalist forces. Aden was temptingly near, just a day's drive through the mountain passes and across the desert flats. Colonel Mahmud Atyia, of Egyptian Military Intelligence, headed an organization to direct dissident operations against the British in 'Occupied South Yemen'. He supervised the training of young tribesmen from protectorate states, and the issue of rifles, machine-guns, mortars and land mines.

In April 1964, Nasser visited some of his 40,000 troops in Yemen and boasted to them that Egypt would 'kick the British right out of the Arab world'.

Dissidents from the Aden Protectorate were drilling in light green uniforms of a new Freedom Army of South Yemen, learning radio techniques, preparing to take the road to Aden when the day came for them to march in to consolidate a 'people's uprising'. The first units of this new army were already in the field, alongside tribal dissidents, harassing British troops. Egyptian agents with arms, cash and promises had stirred up the Red Wolves of Radfan – who wore red paint on their faces – encouraging them to do what they had not dared to do for decades. They had closed the main road from Aden to the Yemen frontier town of Dhala, the route of pilgrim caravans to the holy places of Mecca on which their ancestors had preyed in earlier times.

The Radfan was an area of razor-toothed granite peaks towering 7000 feet over shimmering desert stretching back fifty miles to Aden. Although thirty miles inside the Protectorate it was an area that tribal government by the paramount Sultan of Lahej left alone. No European was known to have entered the area since a missionary disappeared into it around the beginning of World War One.

Now land mines – some stolen from British stores, some supplied by Egypt – added to the natural defences as British forces began a Radfan Campaign to force tribal leaders to accept a treaty of submission to the recently formed Federal Government of South Arabia.

This was, historically, the last colonial war that the British were to fight, and on that account alone it is worth looking at in some detail. The date was 1964. Apart from radios, planes and other modern equipment it might have been set in the imperial past of a hundred years before.

For the first time in these parts the British were up against disciplined men, trained in the use of heavy machine-guns and mortars, professionally directed. Some 2000 British troops were backed by armoured car squadrons, field artillery batteries, sapper units, helicopters and strafing jet planes.

This considerable little war was virtually unnoticed in Britain until the May morning newspaper headlines screamed: 'Two British Soldiers Beheaded'. News reports said that the severed heads of two British soldiers had been put on public display in the Yemen.

This information came from no less a source than Major-General John Cubbon, General Officer Commanding Middle East Land Forces, at a hurriedly called press conference in Aden. It was immediately denied by the Yemen Republic Government, and by the United States consul in Taiz. Such diplomatic relations as Britain had had with Yemen had lapsed because of London's refusal to recognize the Republican Government while royalist armies were fighting it with the overt aid of Saudi Arabian money and arms, and some covert aid from Aden by British intelligence. The US was looking after British interests in Yemen, and the consul in Taiz was reacting to a request from the Foreign Office for confirmation of the military intelligence report of the beheading.

The mystery has never been satisfactorily resolved, and Defence Ministry and Foreign Office archives concerning the affair will not be available till 1994 under the thirty-year secrecy rule.

Two British soldiers, a captain and a sapper, were officially listed 'missing, believed killed'. They were members of a patrol of nine men from the Special Air Service which penetrated deep into the unexplored Radfan to reconnoitre the ground for possible flanking marches into the tribal heartland. The Special Air Service is the military arm of Britain's Secret Intelligence Service and its highly trained, ruthlessly dedicated men are renowned for sealed lips. I interviewed two wounded survivors of this patrol in hospital in Aden with the permission of the highest military officer in the command. They refused to talk to me until their own company officer ordered them to give me some details.

They were dropped into the area by helicopter by night, and moved into narrow wadis around the Wadi Thaim, core of the Radfan, never before penetrated by outsiders. By daylight they lay up close to a village called Shab Tem. They could hear radio chatter from a house obviously used as a headquarters. They counted twenty-two Arabs in khaki uniform jackets, shorts and turbans, carrying rifles.

A wandering goat-herd spotted them and raised the alarm at noon, and heavy and accurate fire from the village and rock spurs around pinned them down, unable to fire back.

Captain Robin Edwards, aged 27, of the Somerset and Cornwall Light Infantry, was in radio contact with operational headquarters seven miles back beside an airstrip at Fort Thumeir. He called in air and artillery support. RAF Hunters caused enemy casualties with pinpoint rocket strikes, but artillery had to cease fire because shells were falling too close to the British position. At dusk about fifty Arabs rushed the SAS position. Captain Edwards, badly hit in the stomach by a burst of automatic fire, ordered Sergeant Reg Lingham to command a break-out leaving him behind. Sapper John Warburton was shot dead. Two men were wounded.

Sergeant Lingham told me as he lay in hospital a few days later,

'We made a run for it, firing as we went at point blank range. I reckon we inflicted thirty casualties. Only three Arabs shadowed us as we made towards our camp at Thumeir. Trooper Baker, wounded though he was, made a stand with two others. They killed one Arab and wounded both others. We kept moving till three in the morning. Then, to avoid being accidentally shot by sentries, we lay up till stand-to and entered camp at 05.30.'

Camp was advanced headquarters, a tented sprawl beside a bumpy four-hundred-yards long airstrip between white-washed Fort Thumeir and the Arab village of Habilayn. The midday temperature was 110 degrees Fahrenheit in the shade, 130 degrees in the sun. All around, ridges of naked rock rose into the shimmering air, fold after fold, towering guardians of the Red Wolves' lair.

Squat on top of a ridge five miles distant was a large fortified Arab house labelled on British army maps 'enemy O.P.'. From this observation post every move in the camp, every arrival and departure of small Twin Pioneer supply planes on the airstrip, every vehicle on the road from Aden could be noted. Permission had been sought for the RAF to 'take out' this enemy eye before final dispositions were taken up for a British invasion of the Radfan beginning at dusk on 4 May.

Just before the air strike was due to go in that afternoon there came a veto from Aden. The rules of minimum force, laid down by the British political authorities for the conduct of military operations in aid of the civil power, forbade firing on habitations. The only exemption was for buildings from which hostile fire had been confirmed beyond doubt. The Aden top brass refused to vary the strict rule – it was not sufficient that tribesmen who had clashed with a British patrol were earlier seen to have come from the fortified watchtower.

The Field Force commander, Brigadier Louis Hargreaves, shrugged at the veto order. The critical part of his attack plan was surprise outflanking of the enemy while he launched a noisy frontal night feint with only a single company of the East Anglian Regiment up the Wadi Rabwa, the direct camel route into the Radfan heartland.

Two razor-edged heights flanking the entrance to Wadi Rabwa had been captured without a shot in a spectacular night march and climb by 45 Commando and an attached company of the Third Paras. Himalayan climber Mike Banks, a company com-

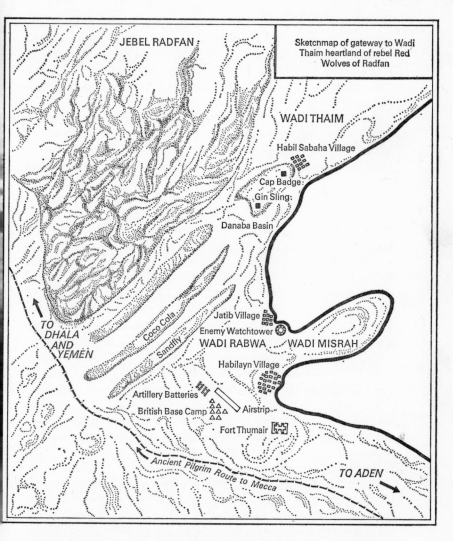

Sketchmap of gateway to Wadi Thaim heartland of rebel Red Wolves of Radfan

JEBEL RADFAN

WADI THAIM

Habil Sabaha Village

Cap Badge

Gin Sling

Danaba Basin

TO DHALA AND YEMEN

Coco Cola

Sandfly

Jatib Village

Enemy Watchtower

WADI RABWA   WADI MISRAH

Habilayn Village

Artillery Batteries

British Base Camp

Airstrip

Fort Thumair

Ancient Pilgrim Route to Mecca

TO ADEN

mander, had led the way. The mile-long ridges ran parallel each side of a deep gorge called the Wadi Boran. The lower one, nearest Fort Thumeir, was code-named Sand Fly, the other Coca Cola.

The main element of the East Anglia Regiment, commanded by Lieutenant-Colonel Jack Dye who figures in a key role later in Aden's story, was to take over Coke Ridge before dusk, while 45 Commando and B Company of the Third Paras pushed forward in a ten-hour night march to establish firm positions on two heights

L.S.–D

dominating the Danaba Basin and the broad Wadi Thaim, the fertile tribal heartland of the Radfan. Because of the reprieved enemy O.P. overlooking the British base positions the Anglians had to make a deceptive detour before doubling back to the ridge. Swathed in bandoliers and sweat the last of them filed into positions already vacated by the commandos.

At dusk one of the helicopters constantly shuttling water – a Gungha Din of the air age – dropped a newsreel cameraman and myself into the Anglian positions on Coke Ridge for a grandstand view of the imminent battle. Shells from batteries of 105 howitzers were already firing the opening stanzas of a rowdy night-long orchestration aimed at covering the outflanking columns snaking through the pitch-black depths of deep gorges. Mortars and machine-guns from our heights joined the barrage. The inky night was holed and perforated with the yellow burst of shells and the red pencil etching of tracer. Sappers of 12 Squadron, Royal Engineers, in the dark depths of Wadi Boran below us, added to the growling thunder of the big guns as they tried to blast a route for Saracen armoured cars of the Royal Tank Regiment to break through into the upper Danaba Valley. Colonel Dye sent down a patrol to follow the route of the Commando march and bring back a man who collapsed with heat fatigue. A droning Shackleton bomber circled all night ready to drop flares if the commandos or Paras called for light.

The sappers ran into impassable rocks and boulders blocking the Wadi Boran for two hundred yards. At dawn the next wadi northwards was reconnoitred and reckoned to be passable, but it was found to run through territory of a neutral sheik who refused permission for the armour to pass.

The main objective of the night marches was a high sharp peak code-named Cap Badge. The Paras marched through the wadi to climb it from its further side. The commandos of X-Ray company, led by Everest Major Mike Banks, were climbing the direct frontal route. Daylight caught both of them still climbing.

The Paras found tribesmen in rock walled gun positions (known as sangars) blocking their way upwards as they began the climb. They also came under heavy fire from a village called Habil Sabaha on the edge of Wadi Thaim. On the nearer side of the ridge X-Ray company was engaged with tribesmen returning to their day-time sniping positions after sleeping in a village.

Lieut-Colonel Pat Stevens, commander of 45 Commando,

secured a near-by peak called Gin Sling as a fall-back position. Meanwhile Zebra Company of 45 Commando was lifted by helicopter from Sand Fly ridge and dropped on to the summit of Cap Badge as bullets flew around the hovering Wessex helicopters of 815 squadron. The commandos moved down from the peak to clear the slopes of tribal snipers.

The Paras had meanwhile charged the village fort and cleared the rest of the village in a fierce hour-long battle. An officer was killed and several Paras were wounded. The tribesmen besieging them were out of range of the artillery batteries at Thumeir and the armoured cars were unable to get through to relieve them. Air strikes by RAF Hunters at low level covered a hazardous drop of water and ammunition by Beavers. A second Briton was killed as the battle continued. Later that afternoon the Paras broke out of the village as commandos charged down from above on the surrounding tribesmen. Ten wounded were lifted out by helicopter. The two dead were buried in unmarked shallow graves as a padre read burial lines, and their commanding officer made a sketch map to assist later recovery of the bodies for proper burial in Aden.

Next day was quiet. Flocks of vultures gathered. Helicopters ferried precious water to the thirsty troops on the Radfan peaks. They also delivered rolls of hessian for the soldiers to rig shelters from the blistering sun. More wounded were flown out to hospital. Already 34 Field Squadron of the Royal Engineers were on their way to build a road into the lair of the Red Wolves of Radfan. Its days of isolation were over.

The Shackleton flew over low in daylight to scatter leaflets warning the tribesmen that those guilty of attacks on government were being punished and all who failed to leave the area must expect attack. The area was under proscription which involves crop burning, removal of livestock, and demolition of fortified buildings.

The hilltop watchtower near Jatib, spared on the eve of the attack, was now fair game because its occupants were known to have fired from it at passing aircraft. I watched two Hunters blow it to pieces. They made twelve runs, four with rockets, eight with cannon.

The Radfan campaign was to continue through May into June, finally bringing the tribes to the British heel in late August. For the remaining phases there were changes of senior command.

Brigadier Hargreaves was replaced by Brigadier Hugh Blacker, just out from Britain, ostensibly to return to his internal security duties in Aden. An unaccustomed spotlight of interest in Britain and the rest of the world was clearly unwelcome. Publicity of the 'right kind' was good for morale, but the whole story in all its controversial aspects was something to be avoided. Changes in the press arrangements made such 'see for yourself' trips as mine a thing of the past. There were no similar facilities for the further progress of the campaign.

The three British fighting battalions established four separate fortress camps dominating the broad Wadi Thaim. Tents were protected by stone walls, and air strips were levelled close by. There was no water shortage. Deep wells supplied two camps and water was ferried from these to the other two. Showers were rigged. Fresh food was flown in from Aden. But they were far from being holiday camps. Cooks and drivers were up every other night on guard duties. Rifle companies were out on patrol every second night. Work on the road was begun.

The tribesmen had dispersed and split into war parties, sniping, laying mines, harassing in guerrilla ambushes. In one fierce clash a combined force of commandos and Paras used ropes to climb down a 2000-foot rock face to surprise a rebel band. An East Anglian patrol camped on the 7000-foot Jebel Huriyah, highest peak in the Radfan, and saw the lights of Aden fifty miles away.

The tribesmen came into the open to fight a pitched battle only once more – on 8 June. It was sheer bravado, and suicidal. The artillery batteries, now moved forward, and the RAF strike planes had never had such a target. British troops watched the butchery before going in to mop up. That was the end of the insurrection.

The campaign closed with what the military laconically termed 'intense application of air control' and constant patrolling. As one military officer put it, 'The effective answer to a tribal rising is to kill so many dissidents that the occupational risks become unacceptable'. By August most of the tribal leaders submitted and agreed to keep the iron-fisted peace Britain's last show of old-fashioned imperial firmness brought to the Radfan. A motor road into Wadi Thaim, providing access to the outer world, is its memorial.

The National Liberation Front of Occupied South Yemen claimed a huge Arab victory. A communiqué issued in Cairo and Beirut claimed that two hundred British soldiers were killed or wounded, eight fighter planes shot down, tanks and armoured cars destroyed and huge quantities of arms and ammunition captured.

While this Radfan Campaign was being fought Russia's leader, Nikita Krushchev, was receiving a hero's welcome in Cairo en route to change the course of the Nile, marking completion of the first stage in building the Soviet Aswan Dam, bigger than the two British-built dams already there.

He made one fleeting, diplomatically restrained comment on events in Southern Arabia in an address to the Egyptian parliament. He said, 'We support the abolition of the slave treaties imposed by Britain to provide excuses for the intervention of troops'.

6 Terrorism Begins

This escalation of tribal disturbances into a major incursion backed by Cairo, with sinister undertones of influence from Moscow and Peking, began to loom forebodingly over the tiffin salons of colonial Aden. An aura of backwater permanency, long settled like dust on archives, began slowly to disperse.

The trade union movement, fostered by earlier colonial administrators, suddenly became a catalyst for every grievance, real and pretended, against colonial rule. The Yemen Fifth Column began to assert itself. A new fever of anti-colonialism, fanned by the anti-British diatribes from Cairo and Sanaa, infected the tiny legislature, forcing the British Governor to suspend it and take direct rule into his own hands.

Seeking a political formula that might secure its last effective military base East of Suez, plus sufficient military influence to prevent a dangerous vacuum in an area on which the industry of the western world was vulnerable, British policy settled firmly on a Federal solution – a full turn of the wheel from the divide-and-rule policy so frequently alleged to be the foundation of British imperial strategy.

The Federal formula – rejected in 1955 – was hawked again around the rulers of the twenty-four protectorate states. A few of the more enlightened – or perhaps more frightened – showed interest. Most repeated objections to any idea of a limit being placed on their despotic whim.

Only six joined together in a Federation of South Arabia in 1959. With an eye to ensuring continued British protection they insisted that Aden Colony must join with the new nation they were trying to form. The notion appealed to colonial officials. A country party might hopefully counterbalance a new breed of urban politician now bidding for power within the colony.

But it was already too late for paternal political and economic progress. The nationalists had the bit in their teeth. British power was waning. It was becoming more and more obvious that the will to rule, the feeling of obligation to wield a world influence, was ebbing away. Nobody was fooled by costly new investment in barracks and installations – £3 millions on RAF facilities at Khormaksar, £300,000 on improvements at Steamer Point, an £8 million new building project at Little Aden.

Fears of the town dwellers that Britain's disciplined garrison might be replaced by desert tribesmen was only one factor in uniting Aden opinion in bitter opposition against the Sultans and Emirs of the Federal Government. There was no love at all for the tribal leaders despite their new-found enthusiasm for a £4 millions grant from Britain for programmes of social reform that created schools and clinics where none had existed before.

The first act of terrorism in December 1963 had been an isolated incident . . . aimed against Aden's link with the Federal Government. A grenade was rolled across the tarmac at Khormaksar airport as the Governor, Sir Kennedy Trevaskis, led a delegation aboard a plane to London for a constitutional conference to confirm the merger of Aden with the South Arabian Federation. It killed an Indian woman in transit from Bombay, fatally wounded the Governor's assistant, George Henderson, as he pushed Sir Kennedy to safety, and delayed the London conference for two months.

Of much more significance to Aden's political future was the result of an election in Britain a month earlier than that first isolated act of outrage. A Labour Government was returned to power in Westminster, although with only a slender majority of five. The empire-minded Duncan Sandys was replaced at the Colonial Office by Anthony Greenwood.

Almost another year passed without incident. Then a visit by Mr Anthony Greenwood brought a flurry of terrorist incidents and organized riots. Most of the attempts were amateurish, but a grenade rolled into the Oasis bar in Maalla killed two British servicemen and wounded fourteen others. Troops blocked roads with coils of barbed wire, searched cars and all 'local nationals' (the military label distinguishing the local population from the ruling race) in the area. From that time all local nationals were automatically terrorist suspects to angry youngsters from Britain.

The good life was over in Aden. Cinemas, nightclubs and bars became places spiced with undertones of peril. Intelligence reports indicated that about two hundred Adenis had received terrorist training from Egyptian agents in the Yemen. Service families began staying at home, or only going out to places of entertainment inside barbed-wire-ringed security areas.

Even within security perimeters danger lurked. On the evening of 23 December 1964, a bomb was tossed among a group of British teenagers dancing the twist in the lounge of an officers' house inside the airport security area. The sixteen-year-old daughter of an Air Commodore, the Principal Medical Officer for Aden, was killed. Several others, including the son of the commander-in-chief, were wounded. That was the thirty-sixth terrorist incident. By this time they were a nightly occurrence.

More battalions of British infantry were flown in for internal security duties in Aden, a tedious, nasty, brutalizing round of patrols and searches and shots in the night.

But it was not without sporting touches and a lighter side. One hot evening in 1965 I went to dinner at the home of a British official in Downing Street, an avenue of spacious modern colonial houses and scene of several bomb incidents. Tribesmen from the personal bodyguard of the Sherif of Beihan were camped among the flowering shrubs under orders to defend their ruler's good British friend with their lives. After dinner we went to see a film entitled 'Zulu' at an open-air cinema in the same residential area. My host, who augmented the security of his tribal bodyguard with a loaded sten gun propped beside his bed, kept a Browning pistol between us on the bench seat of the car. He parked under the close eye of security guards outside the cinema, and tucked the pistol into his trouser top. We sat with backs to a wall in carefully chosen reserved seats.

It proved a rare cinema occasion. The audience seemed fairly evenly divided between young Adenis and off-duty Welsh guardsmen, by coincidence the very same regiment slaughtered by successive waves of Zulu warriors of the earlier colonial troubles portrayed on the screen. Every time a Zulu spear was thrust through a Welsh guards tunic the Arabs yelled and cheered from the well of darkness beneath the screen. Back came voices from the Welsh Valleys, rendering 'Men of Harlech' along with the celluloid heroes, ranks unwavering, on the screen.

All was good natured as though the developing struggle which divided the young Arabs and the young Britons, whether they liked it or not, into enemy camps was just another celluloid story illuminated and moved by the latest model magic lantern.

At this time the ordinary population was far from sympathetic towards terrorist activists. They were aware that the RAF, the primary target of Cairo radio fulminations, daily brought Arabs from remote desert villages for treatment in Khormaksar Beach Hospital, the only hospital in the world run by a military service solely for the care of a backward indigenous population.

The British presence had not yet become symbolized by rough language at gunpoint and manhandling body searches. Sergeant Tony Spargo, of the Army Medical Corps, regularly walked unarmed into the seaside village of Bir Fuqum to open a free clinic. He took the trouble to learn enough Arabic phrases to question his patients about their ailments, and was honoured with the Arab name El Tabib – the one who heals. Other British soldiers built a two-room schoolhouse for girls of the same village.

In Government House and in the new town of Al Ittihad, a Federal capital mushrooming from the desert in an architectural display of modish concrete and glass, there was a feeling of optimism. Nasser's pan-Arab popularity was on the wane. He had promised to throw the Israelis into the sea, and all he had done was commit a huge Egyptian army to a wasting campaign against primitive royalist tribes in the Yemen.

Many Aden workers were still defying frequent calls to strike despite intimidation. Petrol stations stayed open through a petroleum workers' strike to protest against the detention of the union's leader, Mohamed Saleh al Aulaqi, for known association with the National Liberation Front. Just the same the strike succeeded in closing down the airport for the first of many tumultuous strikes soon to become occasions of riot and curfew.

A general strike only weeks later developed into riots. Teenage mobs rampaged through the streets of the Crater district. They piled up barricades, burned old tyres at road junctions, wrecked and burned cars, set fire to the offices of a comparatively moderate

above Anthony Greenwood, then
Colonial Secretary (nearest
window), at a traditional desert
feast.

left Member of sheik's bodyguard.

War dance by tribesmen in Zingabar.

above Nasser bombs on Yemen Royalists.

left British shell Radfan rebels.

Young Britons at war against tribesmen in the Radfan, 1964, the last of Britain's many colonial campaigns.

newspaper, *Al Yaqdha* (Vision). In Bazaar Square a young Arab in a sarong and skullcap told me, 'We shall stand up to the British guns and this place will be called Martyrs' Square. We shall gather here, those who survive, every year on this day and remember our brave brothers who gave their lives for freedom'. This educated young man was obviously revealing an aim of the terrorist conspiracy, and it says much for the discipline of savagely provoked British troops in the closing years of British rule that this dream was never fulfilled.

The only British guns on the spot on this morning were in the hands of the Arab Armed Police, a *gendarmerie* recruited among the desert tribes. Most of them were carrying nothing more lethal than wattle shields and sticks. A teargas canister zipped close by dispersing Arab youths clustered around me listening to my conversation with the young Arab. I was suddenly alone, coughing, face streaming, as I stumbled towards the police line.

'Sorry, sir,' said a British police superintendent. 'But we would prefer you not to hold public meetings just now.'

A cluster of youths chanting 'No base' emerged from a side street and threw jagged pieces of rock our way. Chief Superintendent Arthur Hodges, from Essex, a square-jawed veteran from service in Palestine, stood squarely twenty paces ahead of his men. He raised his teargas gun and fired into the centre of the mob. So it went on throughout the day as mobs ebbed and flowed through the streets and narrow alleyways, splashing through puddles as water gushed from exterior pipes torn down to soothe eyes burning from acrid clouds as scores of teargas canisters showered around the township. Finally the teargas was backed by more lethal measures. The Arab police fired over the heads of the mob and a youth was injured by a ricochet. As dusk approached the police were doing little more than protect firemen damping down blazing cars, and mobs roamed the streets almost at will. British troops were called in for the first time to enforce the curfew. Men of the Prince of Wales Own Regiment fixed bayonets and advanced on the mob. In twenty minutes the streets were clear, and a score or so of the more stubborn rioters were detained in a wire compound in the police barracks. Not one shot was fired by a British soldier.

Little of this tumultuous day was known by the British community, most of whom sat out the strike on beaches, in clubs or at parties on the far side of Mount Shamshan.

While agitation against a British base mounted, surprising things were happening across the wide bay from Steamer Point where the constant flame of a waste gas chimney marked the Little Aden oil refinery. Three miles beyond the oil company's little township, twenty-eight miles by road around the bay from Aden, the desert was a bustle of activity. A new town of novel architectural design was rising from a bleak desert salt pan.

This architectural extravaganza was a new British army canton-ment already named Falaise after the World War Two battle in France. It looked like an upper-income housing estate, built on a budget of £8 millions complete with a church of spectacular structural originality costing £50,000. There were houses for forty officers and 260 other ranks, a shopping arcade, school, library, medical centre to augment the oil company hospital near by, cinema, Olympic-size swimming pool and of course separate clubs for officers and other ranks. Water gushed from deep bore holes to nourish shrubs that were already turning an uninhabitable desert valley into a tropical English garden suburb.

Close by in a lonely desert stretch appropriately named Silent Valley five acres of desert were laid out as a cemetery – a macabre indication of a permanent British presence.

An airstrip close by Falaise had a development potential to take large planes. Deep-water jetties already existed in the oil refinery dockyard. The location, straddling a desert headland, simplified defence from overland attack, and sustenance from supporting naval forces. It was a natural sentinel to the British Petroleum refinery and company town beyond it further along the headland. Little Aden had been hurriedly rebuilt to replace strategic refuelling needs of the Royal Navy, among other reasons, after refineries at Abadan were nationalized during the brief rule of the fiery nationalist agitator Mohamed Mossadegh in Iran in the early fifties. The Little Aden refinery was clearly going to be more difficult to take over in any arbitrary overnight way. Both it and the new military base were built on useless desert land outside the boundaries of Aden Colony, on land obtained by commercial purchase from the tiny sheikdom of Akrabi, smallest state in the South Arabian Federation. Thus a continuing British presence there would be technically beyond the jurisdiction of Aden, a concern of the wider powers held by the Federal Government in Al Ittihad. A continuing British presence after Aden Colony's formal independence would thereby be unobtrusive, unseen in

Aden itself or in any of the populated areas of the federation.

It seemed the ideal answer for a base to continue under the terms of a discreet new treaty relationship with a sovereign South Arabian state. The pattern of such a treaty was already well established. Kuwait's independence had been secured against Iraqi threats of annexation only a few years earlier when British troops were airlifted in under its treaty with Britain. A similar treaty guaranteed Bahrein Island against persistent Iranian claims of ownership. Seven tiny sheikdoms on the south-easterly shores of the Persian Gulf also enjoyed treaties of protection. In these Trucial States Britain directly controlled a *gendarmerie*, the British-officered Trucial Oman Scouts, which policed the desert, and a decade earlier had prevented Saudi Arabian claims to Buraimi Oasis.

The little-publicized building developments at Falaise were nearing completion when the Defence White Paper of February 1966 was published in London. This printed document raised more dust and caused more anxious concern than all the terrorist bombs put together. It amounted to a promise of total British surrender in Aden within two years.

Nasser's flagging interest in Aden took on new impetus. Here was one place an Arab victory could be assured. From this moment stemmed the decision to give the British a send-off with bombs and bullets, and to hell with conferences and documents.

7 Aden on a Platter

Stepping off a plane in Aden during April of 1966 was like entering a Wonderland without Alice. Madhat characters abounded there as the newly announced 1968 deadline for British withdrawal came inexorably nearer each sunset the Union Jack was ceremonially lowered on Flagstaff Hill.

Most astonishing of all was a suspicion, feeding on an element of wishful thinking, that the British were playing a cunning political game – that they really had no serious intention of abandoning the fortress colony. This view was widely held by merchants, government employees, taxi drivers, hotel receptionists, though not by the few politically knowledgeable.

At Checkpoint Bravo, a road roundabout turned into a fortress of sandbagged machine-gun nests and coiled barbed wire, an Arab businessman told me while his car was being searched, 'It is another clever move by the British. They know we shall have to beg them to stay. How can we live without the money the base brings?' Then, hands above his head, he submitted to a body search by a fair-haired soldier of the Coldstream Guards. Other soldiers handed him back his car keys after their thorough search for weapons or explosives.

This was still considered an indignity in those days. Body-searches and baggage checks had yet to become an accepted norm of international travel. It had to be suffered by hundreds of Adenis and their families every time they travelled between their homes in the desert suburb of Sheik Othman and shops and offices in Aden's business areas of Steamer Point and Crater. Most accepted with unprotesting good grace. Good humour often passed between the searched and the alien searcher although roughness and rudeness increased as the scale and callousness of terrorism rose.

The assassination of innocent, unarmed Europeans had become the newest aspect of terrorism in Aden. The murder gangs were finding it dangerous to attack obvious targets like senior government officials, police and special branch officers. They turned instead to cowardly backstreet killings of any European who unwittingly became a target of opportunity.

It was from South Arabia that a Shia Muslim group called the Assassins (Arabic, *Hashashin*) moved into the central stream of Arab politics far to the north a thousand years before. They operated as political 'hit men' in the eleventh century.

The most recent victim of this reversion to ancient ways was a woman passenger in a tourist liner, killed on a morning shopping trip ashore. Because of it only two of some two thousand passengers came ashore from the liner *Orcades* when she stopped briefly in Aden to top up fuel and stores a few days later, and nobody at all ventured ashore from three bunkering merchant ships. The once busy shopkeepers of the Crescent sat amid mountains of duty free radios, cameras and other bric-a-brac of mainly Japanese industry playing trictrac, a version of backgammon.

With the kind of rationality that seems peculiar to the Arab mentality, normally sensible people like airline booking clerks and shipping company officials blamed these illogical killings on devilish machinations stemming from colonial officials in Government House, a place of legend that few Adenis ever got to see even from a distance. The Governor's colonial mansion crowned a clifftop above the reserved beaches of Tarshyne Bay, screened to landward by trees and shrubs, aloof from the sweltering dust of the Crescent shopping area, remote as the Gardens of Eden from the reality of Aden.

The Labour government's decision for total withdrawal was received with disbelief in Government House. Governor Sir Kennedy Trevaskis baulked at putting policies into reverse, and was sacked.

Sir Kennedy lamented later in a book of memoirs (*Shades of Amber*) at the frustration 'of years of effort coming to fruition'. He quoted an Arab leader (unnamed, but clearly Sultan Ali of Lahej) who told him on the eve of defection to Cairo, 'You British always betray your friends. You have done it everywhere.'

British officials went about their tasks like robots, stunned and dejected at the waste of all their efforts to withdraw in good order and leave something better than murderous chaos behind. One of them, a dedicated man who idealized the Bedouin, told me, 'The timing is tragic. Nasser was on his back and on the point of retreat from Yemen. This saves his bacon, and we hand him Aden on a plate.'

President Nasser had already withdrawn the bulk of a 70,000-strong expeditionary force from north and east Yemen to areas closer to the embarkation port of Hodeida when the bland announcement of Britain's total withdrawal from Aden 'before 1968' fell upon an astounded Arab world. Now the Egyptian leader determined to hang on until the British were gone from Aden. In their camps between Taiz and the Red Sea the Egyptian army was poised only a day's drive from the last crumbling redoubt of Britain in the Arab world. Its presence there was sufficiently combustible to create a smokescreen over the real facts of a situation ready made to put over throughout the Arab world as another Nasser triumph over the British.

Nasser was endowed with luck through most of his career as a practitioner of brinkmanship. Something always seemed to turn the running his way when things began to come unstuck. Along with Britain's presentation of Aden on a platter America decided to renew food and aid shipments, by that time desperately needed by an over-extended Egyptian economy.

The traditional rulers designated to succeed the British Raj, equipped with a constitution and a well-trained and well-armed

Federal Army, were naturally in a panic at this prospect of almost instant independence without ongoing sustenance. Especially as it came little more than a year after Anthony Greenwood, Colonial Secretary in the Labour government, personally visited state capitals to renew British pledges. Some of them began to try to mend fences with the terrorist organizations. The long-doubting Emir of Dhala was already known to be making overtures across the frontier despite the proximity of a strong British force in a permanent camp only two miles from his palace.

The RAF flew me up to Dhala for a look at the frontier scene, and I spent a night in Commando Camp, a walled, tented cantonment that had been continuously manned by succeeding units since frontier pressures increased two years before. I wrote the following description at the time:

'The night is dark, moonless. Beneath the shadowy silhouettes of great rocky ridges around us on this last frontier of Empire young Britons stand at the ramparts, watchful, alert, tensed over guns – a lonely garrison in a fortress cut off by many miles of mountain and desert peopled by lawless, hostile tribes. This must have been how it was on the old north-west frontier of India in Kipling's day. Only the weapons, the quality of the rations, the speed of letters from home have changed.

'Keen eyes spotted movement somewhere in the infinity of darkness around. Were Arab rebels stealing barefoot across the rocks to infiltrate the camp?

'A dark figure, peering through binoculars between a split in sandbags, gives a quiet order. The brooding silence ends in a rolling thunder of mortars. Brilliant flares hang suspended on parachutes spotlighting a crag three hundred yards outside the perimeter wire in glaring white light. Red stabs of tracer pencil the darkness. It comes from a flanking picquet lying up on a peak outside the main perimeter.

'The bellow of mortars rumbles around the crags. Cascading explosions splinter the rocks where movement was seen. Suddenly, silence and blackness return. There is no more stealthy movement.

'Major Roy Tuck, commanding X company of 45 Commando, Royal Marines, explains, "We shoot at anything that moves after dark. The entire territory is under dusk-to-dawn curfew".

'Earlier, shells had whistled over our heads to rain harassing fire along a rocky trail, known as the Turkish road, leading from near-by Yemen. They were fired from 125mm artillery of the South

Arabian Army which camped in a similar perimeter near by.

'Major Tuck told me, "The enemy is hard to tell in daytime. Every tribesman older than fourteen carries a rifle. Machine-guns are quite common. We are quite powerless to stop anybody carrying any kind of weapon by day. But at night anybody moving outside his village compound is undoubtedly an enemy."

'Commando Camp is Britain's most forward post on the Yemen frontier – beleaguered except for brief supply visits by Twin Pioneer planes and helicopters. Monthly supply columns coming up from Aden through the twisting passes run a gauntlet of mines and sniping despite a ground escort in battalion strength and over-lapping patrols of low prowling Hunter jet Fighters and armed helicopters. A Sioux helicopter was holed by a bullet only yester-day.

'Every morning at first light a patrol sweeps the track between the camp and the gravel airstrip to clear it of landmines. This morning a mine, presumably fitted with a time fuse, blew a three-foot crater where the morning plane normally unloads the rations. It went off half an hour before the plane came in and hurt nobody.

'Camp Commando has its own Gungha Din. He is honorary Corporal 12345 Willie Smith (real name Arriz Mohamed, aged twenty-six) who warned of a plot to poison the camp's water sup-plies. His loyalty to his British paymasters would cost him his life if he dared set foot outside the camp. Every departing camp commander leaves notes to the relief force commending his loyalty and requesting the newcomers to "look after him well". Now there is concern for his future after the British leave for good.

'Despite this fortress of British power on the edge of his tiny capital the frail-looking Emir of Dhala is virtually a prisoner in his hilltop palace, immaculately white despite sixty or so bazooka shells that have been fired at it. The Emir sleeps in a cellar and employs a full-time plasterer to repair shell holes immediately after each attack. He never moves outside without his bodyguard of thirty, all well armed with machine-guns.

'The Union Jack flies bravely over an old greystone house on the edge of town. There, surrounded by Arab soldiers and a personal bodyguard of two tribesmen, was Stephen Johnson, a twenty-six-year-old bachelor from Billesdon, Leicestershire. He is the political officer, representing Britain, the Emir's protecting power until 1968. Not surprisingly he and his superiors in Aden have lost the Emir's confidence. The Emir is busy with talks with tribal leaders in near-by Republican-held Yemen, men who were his sworn enemies till recently. Just what they talk about he is telling nobody, least of all the British official who till recently was fully in his confidence.

'Stephen Johnson, dressed in flannel bags and open neck shirt, coolly drives his Land-Rover accompanied only by his two tribal guards in places the military hesitate to visit except in force. He told me, "I never doubt their loyalty. I've eaten salt with them and that's enough to put me under the protection of their tribe. My main worry is a rebel called Ali the Giant who has an extremely bold band of about thirty. They push home attacks and are particularly elusive".'

Back in Aden, too, every man's thought now was, like the Emir of Dhala's, concentrated on any means to ensure his own survival. All seven Arab members of the Aden Port Trust announced their resignation.

In every household the agonizing decision had to be made – whether to flee, abandoning homes of a lifetime, or whether to risk staying on into a future that looked bleak, uncertain and dangerous. Most Britons accepted without too much hesitation that they would have to go for good to homes in Britain they knew only as holiday visitors. A few, still short of pension time after a score and more years in Aden, sent home their wives and reckoned they would stick it out.

Wealthier merchants of Indian, Pakistani and Somali origin began sending families back to ancestral homes in the wake of heavy bank transfers. Special ships were being chartered for a mass exodus before the British finally departed. An Arab Deputy Commissioner of Police moved to a security job with the British High Commission in Karachi.

For most of the Arab population the approaching day of liberation was viewed with feelings heavily laced with trepidation.

To the two-year-tour transients of the military garrison it meant no more than a further shrinkage of the horizon, one fewer among the dwindling chances of overseas allowances and homes in the sun.

Military chiefs were openly appalled at the strategic problems facing them without the Aden base, and the power vacuum they feared might tempt Soviet domination of the Indian Ocean and the vital sea lanes between Middle East oil fields and the West.

8 Driving the British into the Sea

Any idealistic expectation that the British government's undertaking to quit Aden by 1968 might end the bloodshed was soon disillusioned. Instead the declaration brought a predictable surge in the tempo of violence as rival terrorist organizations vied in chalking up exploits against the British. It set off a wild scramble to be best placed to grab the reins of power the British were casting away.

President Nasser's agents were backing both main groups, FLOSY (the Front for the Liberation of South Yemen) and the NLF (the National Liberation Front). In broadcasts from Cairo and Sanaa the British decision to quit Aden voluntarily was submerged in a new wave of sabre-rattling . . . the British were on the run . . . Arab patriots must drive them into the sea.

Egyptian arms and money flowed to both FLOSY and the NLF long after it was clear that they were fighting each other more bitterly than they were acting against the British security forces. Nasser, of course, expected that neither would emerge with a strength that might tempt them to show ingratitude for Egyptian help after they took power.

A murderous gang war raged with terrorist bands turning their anti-tank rockets, Czech mortars and Kalashnikov machine-guns against each other. Both contenders showed callous indifference to innocent bystanders. They were hampered only by the intervention of the British security forces in increasingly vain efforts at maintaining law and order.

Ordinary citizens, seeing that the British were intent on deserting them, began to distance themselves from the colonial masters they knew; hopefully, prayerfully choosing the side they expected to take power in a future that held only one certainty – general lack of security for life, livelihood, property and all the familiar certainties of humdrum daily existence that colonialism under the British had meant. Most, had there been a choice, would undoubtedly have opted for the devil they knew.

It developed into a battle between town and desert. FLOSY, dominated by Abdullah al-Asnag's People's Socialist Party, stood for the interests of Aden. The NLF following sprang mainly from the tribal territories, transients of the town, and was led by Marxist extremists in ruthless pursuit of personal ambition.

L.S.–E

Long before the British government's brazen betrayal, the prosperous middle class of Aden had begun to feel that Britain was planning to throw them to the desert wolves, restoring tribal rule over the 'Mecca of wealth' that Aden seemed to desert dwellers. This was when Britain gave way to pressure from the protectorate rulers who argued that the colony must be included in the federation to make it viable. Aden had been railroaded into the South Arabian Federation in March 1963, after years of prevarication and protest from leading townspeople.

Aden people, with their liberal British education, never felt any sympathy for the kind of nationalism that was aimed at bringing them under the repugnant despotic dynasty that ruled Yemen till September 1962. The trade unions failed to win support outside their membership, mainly made up of imported Yemen workers, because unity with Yemen was its main political demand. Adenis still regarded the protectorate rulers in much the same way as they had regarded the Imam. An effective, if somewhat unfair, anti-Federal slogan developed from an argument that if Aden was opposed to Yemen because it was feudal, it was against Federation twenty-six times over. 'Yemen had one despot,' it was said. 'The protectorate twenty-six.'

The timing of the Yemen coup could hardly have been less welcome to the proponents of Aden's merger with the desert states. It removed the major flaw in the emotional appeal for union with Yemen, and made a future with a progressive regime there appear more promising than domination by desert chieftains only reluctantly emerging from feudal ways. To urbanized Adenis federation spelled feudalism.

Overnight Abdullah al-Asnag, Secretary-General of the TUC, most forthright critic of Aden's merger with the infant Federation of South Arabia, became the dominant political figure outside the colonial establishment.

Back in the summer of 1962 Asnag, then twenty-seven, with the help of three barristers, formed the People's Socialist Party. His use of trade union strikes as a political weapon became part of the pattern of colonial life, and he became widely regarded as a coming First Minister in a self-governing Aden. Colonial officials expected that he would come round to realize the workers had a vested interest in the prosperity of the harbour and this would tame his wilder flights of fancy about union with Yemen and the United Arab Republic. One of history's tragic might-have-beens (though still no has-been in Arab politics) Asnag might well have succeeded in presiding over a smooth transition from outdated colonialism to a happier independence a decade earlier or a decade later. But at that time moderation in politics was out of style. It was never an Arab characteristic anyway.

Britain was by this time committed to the South Arabian Federation with Aden merged into it. To British officials this seemed likely to secure the future of a base as an inherent feature of a treaty of protection with the new state. A base on long lease was regarded as more semantically acceptable than anything like sovereign base areas as retained in Cyprus. Aden's merger was a *fait accompli* when Labour came to power with its hasty decision to scrap all commitments East of Suez.

Asnag first went to jail under the Industrial Relations Ordnance, then into exile. He was fundamentally a non-violent moderate, pushed to some extent by the wilfulness of some British officials, mainly on the tide of Arab nationalism into the ranks of men whose first political belief was the Maoist dogma that power springs from the barrel of a gun.

It was strange to meet the tubby salon extremist, son-in-law of an Indian millionaire merchant, who earlier moved confidently through colonial society, at his terrorist headquarters in Taiz, the twin Yemen capital at the end of the desert road from Aden. When we met there in March 1967, he was clearly unhappy at women and children being caught up in the mayhem in Aden. He rationalized violence as 'unfortunately necessary' in order to prevent Britain succeeding with plans to hand power to the tribal rulers who would wield it ruthlessly, ending all hope of democratic self-government. He said, 'We hate killing, but violence is the only way left to prevent the British maintaining their influence through a puppet regime of unrepresentative and unpopular sultans'.

His office was on the third and top floor of a small apartment block taken over as FLOSY headquarters. It was close by Egyptian military headquarters, and the area around was teeming with Egyptian paratroopers. I had been escorted across the desert and mountains from Lahej, just beyond the last British check-point, by a former colonial office employee, an Arab who now carried a steel blue automatic in his waistband. Asnag sat beneath portraits of President Nasser and Yemen's President Sallal. He claimed that FLOSY alone was fighting to kick out the British and their stooges, and that people who claimed to fight under the NLF label were traitors in the pay of British Intelligence.

Among those who had forsaken the rule of so-called British stooges to join the growing band of FLOSY exiles in Cairo and Taiz was Aden Colony's last Chief Minister, Abdul Qawi Mackawee, a former senior executive in Aden's biggest merchant company, owned by a French family with interests also in Djibouti, trading under the name of Best and Company. Mackawee had stormed aboard a plane to exile in Cairo exclaiming, 'The British have lost their senses' after Sir Richard Turnbull, the High Commissioner (the rank of Governor was dropped when Aden merged into the Federation) sacked his government for refusing to condemn terrorist murders. From that time Aden was under the personal rule of the incumbent in Government House, acting for the Colonial Office in London, until the final British withdrawal.

Shortly after Asnag's denial that a rival NLF existed Mackawee's twenty-one-year-old niece, Nagwa, was arrested for distributing NLF leaflets, and with cruel irony Mackawee's three sons died when a bomb, planted by the NLF, shattered the exiled former Chief Minister's home in Aden.

Many old scores were settled in the guise of political killings that by now had made murder a commonplace. It was not a time to be owed large sums of money or to be privy to other men's secrets.

The Federal Defence Minister, younger brother of the ousted exile in Cairo, was blown up by a land mine as he drove to his office. He escaped with multiple injuries. Sultan Nasser bin Abdullah was deposed as ruler of Wahidi state in the Eastern Protectorate after his arrest for planting a bomb in a plane that killed his own brother and twenty-seven others on an internal flight. The Secretary-General of the South Arabian League was wounded in an ambush in Maalla a few days after escaping the arson of the League's club and offices in Crater. Employees of Aden Airways, a hotbed of Asnag followers from the time he himself was chief reservations clerk, were shot down one after another in systematic liquidation. Terrorists were not safe from rival murder attempts even in British detention cells. The prison at Al Mansoura, where most were held, was the target of a bazooka attack.

The gangs helped themselves to funds from the district

branches of banks, evacuated by British staff, but supposedly under the protection of Arab Armed Police.

A visual graph of the progress of the power game was displayed on walls and rock faces in every part of Aden. By Easter 1967 there were few bare patches. Most FLOSY slogans had been obliterated and the NLF clearly dominated the wall scrawls.

The NLF was led by faceless men. It had no known leadership, and British intelligence, often accused of sponsoring it as a secret arm against FLOSY, seemed to have little idea about it. It was uncannily well informed about British moves, and reasons for this became clear when its leadership was eventually revealed. Its political philosophy, such as it was, was clearly out of step with Nasser's brand of Arab socialism. It was vaguely Marxist, strongly influenced by the terrorist cult martyr of the time, the famous Cuban guerrilla Che Guevara, in contrast to the silk-suited figure of President Nasser, invariably pictured wearing a smart collar and tie which was regarded by NLF fighters as a uniform worn by lackeys of capitalist imperialism. NLF prisoners provided little information. They knew only their immediate associates.

Egyptian Military intelligence headquarters at Taiz formed a new hard-core murder organization in a desperate attempt to counter the NLF's liquidation of FLOSY. It was called PORF – the People's Organization of Revolutionary Forces. It put nine gangs into the embattled streets of Arab areas where – except in Crater – British troops by this time rarely ventured. Some of the Sultans were believed to be behind yet another murder gang called the Avengers.

The Federal Information Minister, burly, handsomely grey-haired Abdul Rahman Girgirah, an Adeni, made a dramatic Churchillian effort to shake the long-intimidated bulk of the Arab population into seeing the threat hanging over them.

Mr Girgirah, already high on the terrorist execution list, taunted his fellow citizens in Arabic, 'Do you think that by tamely lying down to this bullying terrorism we shall avoid the fate that has befallen our brothers in Yemen? No, we must show these cowards and traitors, these servants of Egyptian oppression, that our patience is at an end. We must purge our land of this Egyptian pestilence.'

He voiced the question every ordinary citizen was asking himself in despair.

'Why are men murdered, families terrorized, property destroyed?

It can't be to get the British out. They are going anyway. It is because of orders from Egypt that everything dear to us must be destroyed in order to create chaos and fear so that we will fall easy victims to Egyptian imperialism from the very day we receive our independence.'

9 Necessary Perfidy

Britain was now truly on the horns of a savage dilemma. Her interests, as laid down by current government policies and realistic attitudes to a diminished status among the leading military powers, dictated an end of direct involvement in the affairs of distant lands, and especially a need to end the colonial status of the troublesome enclave on the tip of the Arabian Peninsula.

The mischievous interventions of President Nasser had sabotaged any real chance of a tidy hand-over leaving behind a continuance of basic law and order under a Federal Government, howbeit far from ideal as an example of democratic rule. The worst that disappearing prospect might have had in store for the general population of Aden was a downgrading from the most politically developed community in the Arabian peninsula to either a right wing autocracy or rule by an army clique. Neither would have been any worse for the ordinary Arab, whether workman or student or shopkeeper, than living in Jordan, Saudi Arabia or Kuwait – and materially, at least, considerably better than countries ruled by left wing military juntas of political elitists as in Egypt, Syria and Iraq where squabbles over top power, economic experiments and rigid controls bred wider frustration and poverty.

Nasser's trouble-stirring was compounded incalculable times over by the astonishing blunder of announcing a time limit for Britain's total withdrawal, lock, stock, powder keg and protective cover from commitments bestowed by history. The guilty were those in Westminster who so thoughtlessly dismissed Aden as a mere colonial hangover to be discarded as quickly and discreetly as possible. It threw away every bargaining counter that might have brought the most recalcitrant nationalists to a conference table to iron out a broadly representative agreement for the territory's future. Reducing actions that affected the lives of many thousands, caused the deaths of thousands, to mere gambling terms . . . this naïve advance notice of good intentions revealed the hidden cards that might have been played with more honour to Britain, and might have won a better future for a community raised by Britain.

The bland British announcement in Parliament in February 1966, that British troops would be withdrawn from Aden by 1968 – especially the unexpected rejection of any kind of defence commitment to the new state after independence – shook friend and foe alike throughout the Arab world. Britain's numerous admirers, a silent minority in most Arab countries, were incredulous; the new transistor generation of Britain-baiting demagogues were delirious. Few, if any, Arabs were prepared to give Britain any kudos for honest, good intentions.

In Aden it was seen as a death-knell to prospects that a Federal Government, backed by a disciplined army capable of suppressing the terrorist gangsters, would enable life and reasonable good order to continue.

Nobody was more sickened than the man who ruled over the colonial regime, High Commissioner Sir Richard Turnbull. He had long been at loggerheads with Mr George Brown, the Labour Foreign Secretary, often described by colonial officials as 'Nasser's pen pal'. As a primary assassination target Sir Richard was penned within the secure inner perimeters around Government House on a clifftop headland. Most of his personal staff carried revolvers as did most Europeans in Aden. Sir Richard kept a home-made catapult beside his papers, venting his spleen on crows attempting to raid flower beds on his terrace. On rare visits outside this ivory tower of isolated power he travelled by helicopter in order to reduce hazards to families living along the roads he would otherwise have had to use. Shortly before the political bombshell from Whitehall an attempt to kill him was thwarted by the discovery of a land mine beneath a helipad at the Federal capital of Al Ittihad only minutes before his helicopter was due to land.

Since suspending the constitution and dismissing the government of Abdul Quawi Mackawee for terrorist sympathies in September 1965, he had ruled Aden himself from his wide desk in Government House. He was no stranger to terrorism having served in Kenya as Minister of the Interior during the Mau-Mau troubles. Now he faced the wrath of Arabs who had stood up to be counted as Britain's friends – people who now felt themselves betrayed by a British government that sought to wash its hands of the whole dirty business in Aden by complete abdication of responsibility. It was a shameful position for a greying, bespectacled man of fifty-seven, whose life had been spent serving the Imperial tradition.

Britain was unilaterally abrogating solemn treaties of protection that specifically ruled out any changes without mutual consent. Only a decade before a Sultan of Lahej had been deposed for trying to end his treaty relationship with Britain unilaterally and joining Egypt and Syria in their brief attempt at forming a wider United Arab Republic.

Britain's perfidy was broken to leaders of the Federal Government a few days before the public announcement in Parliament. Lord Beswick flew out to tell a gathering of the rulers, men who topped the terrorist execution lists as 'lackeys of Britain', that they were to be left to their fate.

One of them, Sultan Saleh bin Husein Al Audhali, Minister of Defence in the South Arabian Federal Government, replied, 'The whole Arab world will regard us as fools for having placed so much reliance on the solemn promises of the British government.'

He argued that Britain was treaty-bound to protect the new state until it was ready to defend itself and end the old treaties of protection with Britain by mutual consent.

He added, 'It is said that the British government's decision is based on a need to economize. You must understand you are economizing at the expense of the lives and property of other people.'

Pointedly he said, 'We believe the campaign of attacks and subversion will be stepped up so that it will be made to appear to the world as if Britain had been driven into the sea. We fear this will reach its peak at the very moment of Britain's abandonment of us.'

The brutal fact was that the treaties were hangovers from another era, from times when the *Pax Britannica* was a blessing to millions of diverse peoples around the world. Imperialism had become a dirty word. The sun had set on British global power from the time of the shamefully hurried withdrawal from India two decades before. It never really recovered from the humiliating triumphs of the Japanese in the initial stages of the Pacific struggles in the Second World War.

Unfortunately the world has produced nothing to replace the imperial British role of maintaining law and order over large areas of the world, suppressing slavers and murderers and thieves whether they operated as mere robber bands or as ambitious tribal chieftains, the earliest users of nationalist sentiment for private gain.

The United Nations Organization had a fine opportunity of establishing a deterrent against gangsterism sheltering behind national sovereignty, as recently most spectacularly displayed in Uganda, in the Congo (now Zaire) when Belgium abandoned its vast colonial museum-piece in overnight huff in 1960. It was a spectacular failure. Many of its national contingents, most noticeably the Egyptian, betrayed the UN blue berets in brazen service of orders from Cairo aimed at furthering Nasser's ambitions.

Here again in Aden a situation was developing that needed the purposeful intervention of a world-backed police force to maintain peace and order for the average citizen while contending political ambitions were squared off by peaceful negotiation.

The British government, helpless in the face of Arab refusals to sort out their differences around a conference table, turned to the United Nations. The idea was to get the terrorist leaders to a conference table to negotiate a broader-based caretaker government to whom Britain could hand over. This would provide a government that could be seen not to be a British puppet regime.

Mr George Thomson, Minister of State at the Foreign Office, visited Aden to persuade the Federal rulers to share government with leaders of FLOSY and the NLF.

He also carried from London the British government's cold rejection of demands made by a Federal Mission to London the week before. This had urged postponement of independence for two years, till 1970. It also asked for British troops to stay to defend the frontiers against invasion by Egyptian and Yemen troops until the Federal Army was sufficiently trained in its new equipment to take over, and a Federal air force was formed. At least, they had pleaded, guarantee British aid against an external attack.

There were no doubts at that time about the Federal Government's ability to handle the internal security situation. Federal Ministers often boasted how much tougher they would be when British rules for 'minimum force' no longer applied. They would not worry about repercussions in other Arab countries whose governments ruthlessly suppressed any dissent.

There were still no qualms about the loyalty of the Federal armed forces to the established government. Their smart British-style bearing and drill made any likelihood of politics in the army all but unthinkable!

Mr Thomson was badly received. The old Sherif of Beihan, once so fiercely proud of his alliance with the British 'defender of the faith', refused to meet with the representative of the perfidious socialist government in London. The meeting was long and heated and the Federal Ministers refused to agree to British plans for a General Election under United Nations supervision for the formation of a provisional government to negotiate independence.

They also refused to be associated with an agreed date for Aden's independence. It was, remember, only the seventy-five square miles of Aden that Britain was making independent. It never held sovereignty over the states of the hinterland.

Britain wanted Aden Independence Day to be some time late in November, and insisted it should be no later than the second or third week in January 1968. Any postponement beyond that, Mr Thomson said pointedly, was 'logistically inconvenient' as the British rearguard was to be taken off immediately the Union Jack came down for the last time.

The British minister flew back to London without breaking the deadlock after warning Federal Ministers, 'It is Britain's right and duty to decide the date if no agreement is possible'.

The British haste to leave ahead of its own 1968 deadline was partly based on worries that Arab soldiers of the Federal Army, due to take over internal security duties in Aden itself in the autumn, might be involved in a bloodbath while Britain still held nominal sovereignty and responsibility.

Mr Thomson had arrived on a 'Lollipop Special', a flight packed with boys in school blazers, girls hugging dolls or tennis rackets, part of a swarm of British children arriving to spend Easter holidays with parents.

In a splendid display of phlegm worthy of Drake and his bowls on Plymouth Ho the British were about to make the most of the golden beaches behind the security fences to take a last family holiday in Aden.

Meanwhile Arab terrorists were ready to give the British forces what they boastfully promised would be a week of hell to coincide with a visit by a United Nations delegation.

10 Lovely War – For Some

The headline 'Oh, What a Lovely War' above a picture of tanned soldiers lolling beside an Aden swimming pool carried a certain truth. Planes brought children out each school holiday to join their parents for long days of beach idling, surf bathing and enjoyment of facilities better than any commercial holiday camp could provide. The degree of risk from a terrorist bomb or grenade varied from the practically nil upwards largely depending on the situation of the temporary home in Aden. Those who lived in the cantonment areas around the elegant villas of senior civil and military officials on the rocky headland of Steamer Point had little to worry about. The secure beaches were in this area. Those with homes within the Khormaksar base sprawl were still able to wander about without fear within the perimeter wire, but had to run the gauntlet of Maalla's grenade alley to reach the secure beaches. It was much less fun to live in the sun, coddled by servants, subsidized by duty-free shopping, for those families in the high rise apartments on both sides of Maalla and beside the Queen Arwa Road in Crater.

In happier times these last were able to get to know something more of the strange environment around them than the families aloof from the real Aden in the pockets of English suburbia within the cantonments. They picked up a smattering of Arabic, made Arab friends, played darts with young Arabs in bars.

This relationship was one of the early targets of terrorist gangs as the tossing of grenades into bars like the Oasis on Maalla, where Britons and Arabs drank together, showed. Life for the families 'outside the wire' became increasingly taut as the terrorist campaign gathered momentum. Their homes became fortresses, sweltering prison cells to wives and children through long nights and frequent daytime curfews. The apartments were barricaded and turned into high-rise cantonments, guarded by off-duty servicemen taking turn at stints as block wardens. The windows of white painted school buses were covered with wire grilles to ward off hand grenades and armed soldiers rode shotgun beside the driver. Husbands carried guns to escort wives out shopping. Every afternoon and weekend those who could escaped to the secure beaches at Tarshyne, unperturbed by the rumbles of trouble across the volcanic ridges in Crater where the Northumberland

Fusiliers were carrying the main brunt of street rioting and grenade attacks.

The Geordies were, as the army jargon has it, 'unaccompanied' by families, being on a one-year assignment for special internal security duties. Most of the regular garrison, on posting with families, had desk jobs.

Few service families lived in Crater, simply because it was the hottest, ugliest district in a generally harsh landscape. Those who did stayed on in apartments lining one side of the Queen Arwa Road while frantic pleas for safer billets elsewhere were ignored. The last were evacuated only weeks before Crater's brief period of premature independence in June.

Among the few British civilians who chose to make a home there was Bill Figg, a jolly eighteen-stone Sussex man who had run a bakery in near-by Zaffaran Street for fifteen years. He was confident he had no enemies among his Arab neighbours and refused to abandon his home even after two grenades exploded on his terrace, fortunately while the house was empty. In March 1967 he was shot dead in the street outside the bakery, one of the first victims of a stepped-up murder campaign that virtually declared an open season for shooting any white face. The NLF claimed the jolly baker was executed as an intelligence informer. His shooting followed attempts to wipe out the heads of British Intelligence in bomb and grenade attacks on their homes. The wives of two special branch men were killed and eleven other guests were wounded at a buffet dinner party. A bomb exploded under a settee on which the women were sitting. Their husbands had phoned to say they would be delayed a little longer at the office.

Ali Abdu Gabir, aged twenty-five, servant of the government family hosting the party, disappeared shortly after serving pre-dinner drinks. His picture was circulated on a wanted poster, and a warning leaflet went out to families asking 'Do you really want a servant?' Most of the memsahibs, whether they came from Windsor or Wapping, felt they did and were prepared to risk treachery rather than give up the services of cooks and ayahs (children's nurses), most precious of the dwindling perks in the disappearing colonial way of life.

Two nights later a grenade was tossed on to the terrace of an officer's villa in Waterloo Lines, within a ten foot perimeter fence dividing British homes from the Arab army's Lake Lines cantonment. Three senior military intelligence officers and their wives were having coffee after dinner. Six of the ten people at the party were wounded.

A vigilance leaflet was issued listing thirteen basic precautions against attacks by gunmen and grenade throwers, the emphasis on each being to regard every Arab with suspicion, though the leaflet put it more delicately. The same week two armour-piercing mortar bombs were fired indiscriminately into a block of apartments on Maalla. Nobody was seriously hurt as they smashed into the steel shutter of a ground floor shop and blasted a two-foot hole in the empty lounge of a service family dining out with friends.

Meanwhile normal violence continued on the streets. A typical summary of weekend incidents in February listed forty-five grenade attacks, fourteen shootings, two mortar attacks, the defusing of a land mine and three pipe mortar bombs; the capture of nine grenade throwers and one gunman, nine local nationals killed and twenty-three wounded. Thirteen members of the British forces and sixteen policemen were wounded, 287 local nationals were in detention. Most of the wounded local nationals – a label covering all non-Europeans – were innocent passers-by. The Monday morning these figures were released four Arabs were killed and another six injured by a grenade that bounced off a British armoured car in a crowded street. The grenade thrower was shot dead. About the same time Mr George Brown, then Foreign Secretary, was telling the House of Commons that things were quieter than normal in Aden!

It was against this background, plus fears that a visit by a United Nations mission would create new dimensions of violence, that parents were officially advised to abandon plans to bring children from school in Britain to join them in Aden during the Easter holidays. Most ignored the advice. More than four hundred children arrived in BOAC planes popularly known as 'Lollipop Specials'.

The argument seemed reasonable: three thousand children, mostly under nine, were already living in Aden, attending military schools. Why shouldn't elder sisters and brothers join them? Again it largely depended on the location of the family home in Aden. Only within the perimeter wire of Steamer Point headland was it totally secure.

Despite its old reputation as a penal station for regiments disgraced in battle or officers involved in scandal, despite being one of the hottest, most humid places on earth, Aden was not without its attractions. The desert interior, for the rare few who saw anything at all outside Aden's borders, is a microcosm of storybook Arabia in scenery and customs. Within the colony the towering crags around Crater and the remoter parts of Steamer Point held a wild beauty, particularly at sunrise or sunset. But for the majority the sun-bathing, surfing, sports opportunities, the clubs, the drinking and the dancing parties, with the recent key element of air conditioning, deep freezing and yesterday's London newspapers – often even the same morning's paper – took the sweltering boredom out of a posting there.

Easter holidays passed happily for the families on Tarshyne beach. The heavy surf drowned all save the bigger bangs of the fury across the ridges in Crater and in more distant Sheik Othman. They read about it in day-old papers from London, or heard it on the World Service of the BBC. To many in Aden it was as unreal – something happening to somebody else somewhere else – as it was to readers of the same newspaper stories in England.

Soon after the 'Lollipop Specials' took the children, happily all unscathed, back to Britain, evacuation – euphemistically termed rundown – of British service families began in earnest. It was scheduled to lift out seven hundred and fifty wives and children a week so that all would be gone before the summer holidays. In June, when the security situation deteriorated rapidly, the tempo was doubled. Airliners brought in troop reinforcements and carried back some of the remaining 2300 wives and children at just a few hours' warning to pack for home. At the same time emergency plans were made to evacuate 1500 wives and children of British civilians employed in government, oil refining, shipping, banks. Men whose jobs were not vital were also advised to leave.

Civilian wives, spearheaded by wives of some senior government officials, held meetings to protest against the evacuation order. One wife complained, 'The evacuation order came right out of the blue. This is a British colony for another six months after all.'

A ship from Bombay picked up a thousand departing Indian families settled in Crater since the earliest British days and mountainous piles of luggage.

Among wives faced with a hurried exit were women whose lives were spent in Aden between annual leave at home in Britain. Mrs Daphne Duncan, wife of a shipping agent, had lived in Aden for thirty-seven years. She was a girl of five when her father joined the Aden Port Trust. She lived in a spacious bungalow, shaded by screens of brilliant flowering plants. Around this civilian home the military octopus had spread tendons on every side with Middle East Command headquarters on the ridge above, a sergeant's mess down the road, and ambulances all too often racing up the hill to the RAF hospital. It was, of course, as secure as any place could be in Aden, tucked behind the same security defences as military headquarters and Government House.

Mrs Duncan was not at all reluctant to be leaving. Her main worry was leaving her husband behind at an office in the Crescent, stalking ground of a lone Arab assassin whose toll of European victims was already in double figures.

An Arab house-boy served cold beer as she said, 'One would need to be mad to want to stay in such chaos, but I'm very sad for the Aden I knew until just a few years ago. People always found it hard to believe we enjoyed living here. But all we lacked was winter sports. It really was a good life and the local people were so friendly.'

She recalled, 'In 1930 it was a small, a neat, a happy place. There were not many officials, not many troops. We had thunderboxes for toilets and ice came every day in big packing cases.'

She paused, 'Now it's such a shameful mess, and I blame British wavering and lack of determination as much as anything else.'

(Mrs Duncan was private secretary to former governor, Sir Kennedy Trevaskis, when the idea of forming the desert tribal states of the hinterland into a federation was first mooted.)

She knew Aden only during school holidays in the early years, then served in Aden as a member of the Wrens (Women's Royal Naval Service) during the war and was demobilized in the colony. It was then she met her husband Ian, just out of the Indian Army and beginning a career in shipping. They married in the tiny, redstone church at the bottom of the hill from their home, and honeymooned in a little house twenty miles out in the desert which was loaned to them by an Arab friend. Then it was a deserted area of salt flats and untrodden beaches. It had since become the oil refinery town of Little Aden. Their daughter was born in the RAF hospital up the hill, but was spending holidays in England this summer instead of jetting home to Aden for a holiday from secretarial college in Tunbridge Wells. 'She was furious at being told not to come. She loves it here though a close friend was killed by a grenade thrown into a Christmas party three years ago.'

Mrs Duncan's immediate worry was her eight-year-old dachshund, Trudy, mother of twenty-two. 'I want to have her on my knee for the flight home, but I'm told pets are not allowed on George Brown airlines.'

While all this was going on the majesty of the law, British-style, was being upheld. A senior British adviser to the Federal Government was fined £25 by an Indian magistrate in court at Al Ittihad, the Federal Capital, for firing warning shots into sand at the feet of two Yemeni workmen who trespassed in his garden. The British prosecutor said the court should take a serious view of careless use of arms by people allowed to carry weapons simply because of the emergency.

A twenty-year-old British soldier lingered for months in prison under sentence of death for murdering a taxi driver while off duty in civilian clothes. Although Britain had abolished the death penalty in the UK Aden's colonial legislature had done nothing about its repeal. The East African Court of Appeal, which dealt with cases from courts in various Commonwealth and colonial territories, had rejected his appeal. He was eventually discreetly reprieved by the Foreign Secretary, and returned to Britain to serve an alternative prison sentence.

But trial by jury was suspended as inoperable because of intimidation of jurors in pending cases against terrorists.

One NLF executioner was caught seconds after he had shot bound hostages of the FLOSY faction, but his trial was abandoned because due process of law was simply overwhelmed by the rush of events. Towards the end hard core detainees were being released because of overcrowding in cells. One was a police inspector caught with arms and ammunition hidden in his car.

Anarchy was already taking over.

11 Tragic UN Pantomime

In the earliest tradition of Aden's boisterous politics a general strike was called to coincide with the visit of the United Nations mission. Both FLOSY and the NLF, being opposed to any solution that involved less than exclusive power in their own hands, called for a total boycott of the three-man mission, chosen from the UN's notoriously prejudiced Committee on Colonialism. The committee had already denounced the Federal Government as lackeys of British Imperialism. The task of the men from Mali, Afghanistan and Venezuela, sent by the UN to Aden, was to recommend practical steps for the territory's decolonization.

While they dallied a week in Cairo on their journey to Aden the terrorist gangs had ample time to prepare a campaign of riot and bloodshed aimed at demonstrating that the colonial British were hanging on in Aden by means of violent military repression. Two-and-a-half thousand front-line troops from Britain were at a state of readiness to meet the challenge. Another seven thousand stood guard on British installations and family quarters.

Any forlorn British hope that the mission members might rise above the prejudiced, preconceived debating claptrap of their normal habitat, and make a serious effort to co-operate in resolving the situation on the ground in Aden as they saw it, was quickly dispelled.

A final attempt at a generally acceptable constitution, newly drawn up by two British experts, was hardly looked at, certainly given no serious consideration.

A modern edifice called the Seaview Hotel, rising in a haze of bilious green concrete above Khormaksar beach, was turned into a fortress to house the UN mission for an expected three-day stay. It was along the eastern shore of the Aden peninsula, half a mile from the Lower Pass into Crater, core of the unrest. They landed at a helipad laid out specially in the playground of neighbouring apartments from which British service families were hurriedly evacuated on the eve of their arrival. An RAF helicopter carried them from the airport two hours after dusk – an alarming trip as the pilot took evasive action to avoid tracer bullets, fired from Sheik Othman, that danced around them.

Reporters were barred from the airport on grounds of tight security, and kept out of the Seaview Hotel by the Aden Armed Police backed by a bodyguard of security guards from New York headquarters wearing UN uniform. The only Briton involved in the hotel's security was Deputy Superintendent Len Lack of the Armed Police. He was suspended from duty on what was termed 'unrecorded leave' after the first night. The police commissioner told him he might be shot by his own men if he went back to the Seaview. That ominous portent was swept discreetly under Government House carpets, instead of being interpreted as an early warning of treachery soon to follow.

Two factors combined to postpone the all-out terrorist offensive planned to begin with the mission's arrival, although a general strike was already paralysing all normal activity. One was a British Intelligence coup that brought the biggest terrorist arms haul to date from a raid on a house in Sheik Othman. The other was a downpour of two-and-a-half inches of rain the day before that had flooded streets knee deep, saturating ammunition and explosives along with the possessions of innocent people. Carpets and blankets were put out to dry on every terrace and window balcony.

The Arab Armed Police barracks, beside the Queen Arwa dual carriageway, was decked with cartridge bandoliers hung in the sun to dry off. For the only time in living memory the ancient water conservation tanks, repaired by the first British settlers, were brimming over. Such rain – as much in this one downpour as had fallen over several previous years – was seized upon by the superstitious as an augury for a better future. But the hot sun soon steamed Aden tinder dry again.

First thing on the Monday morning after the UN arrival Sir Richard Turnbull, normally a stickler for the niceties of behaviour, brushed aside all normal protocol. Instead of waiting for the visitors to make the customary courtesy call on him he flew from Government House in a helicopter, studiously avoiding the direct route across Crater, to welcome the UN trio in their hotel.

As his helicopter landed in a swirl of sand beside Seaview, mobs barricaded the back streets of near-by Crater and lit huge bonfires of rubber tyres. The campaign, aimed to prove to the UN investigators that the British were brutally suppressing a popular revolution, was opening.

The UN mission itself was set on following its own rigid protocol. Sir Richard was told bluntly that they were prepared to deal with Britain through its officials as the administering power, but would have nothing to do with members of the Federal Government. They were on firm ground legalistically. Britain, as protecting power for the inland states, was legally responsible for their external relations. Minds were directed to a search for a formula that would enable the mission to have dealings with members of the Federal Government without bestowing recognition on the Federal Government. This was necessary for the mission to travel outside Aden where the Federal Government was everywhere legally responsible for internal law and order. By this date most British forces had already been withdrawn into the Aden perimeter. Only specialized units giving logistical and technical support to the Federal Army were still up-country, mainly in the Dhala area where the threat of 'foreign invasion' was centred.

An RAF plane was on special stand-by to fly the mission anywhere its members wished to go throughout the tribal areas – with a second available to carry the press if the mission went against normal United Nations secretiveness and invited publicity. The Federal Defence Minister, Sultan Saleh, had fifty sharp-shooters from his own Audhali state as a travelling bodyguard. A battalion of the Federal Army had been specially trained to British infantry standards to secure areas in which they chose to travel.

But the mission showed no enthusiasm for up-country touring, and surprised Sir Richard and his staff by announcing that they would stay only eight days in Aden. It seemed that their long stop-over in Cairo had persuaded them that FLOSY was the wave of the future in Southern Arabia.

The talks were adjourned to Government House where they stayed for lunch before returning to the Seaview to deliberate. Nothing more was heard of them for forty-eight hours. They stayed inside the Seaview Hotel, seeing nobody.

Earlier they had complained that the RAF Wessex helicopter, assigned to transport them more securely than driving through the streets, was smelly and the windows were too small to see what was happening below.

Sir Richard sent them a case of his champagne; the Government House information adviser, A. C. Ashworth, loaned them his transistor radio and a pile of paperbacks for the UN guards. A film projector, screen and reels of a western were also sent to Seaview.

Only a new surge in violence, epicentred in the near-by Crater district, intruded noisily on their seclusion. During day-long Sunday riots there were seventy shootings and grenade incidents – a new record for one day.

Terrorist tactics were to use mobs to draw British troops into the narrow streets around Main Bazaar Road where snipers and grenade throwers lay in ambush on balconies, roof tops and in the minarets of mosques. Carried out by bolder, more resolute men against soldiers less meticulously trained than the Northumberland Fusiliers, British casualties would have been serious. As it was most snipers' bullets missed and the jagged hot metal of grenades passed harmlessly over alert soldiers flattened on the pavement at the first sharp warning call 'grenade'. But not all. Eight British were wounded. Two Arabs were killed, eleven wounded.

This was the kind of cold statistic on which one of the transitory pundits of the Sunday newspapers, aloof from the blood and guts in the street, described dangers faced by British youngsters as 'extravagant and harmless gun battles that are such a noisy feature of the Aden scene'. American correspondents, whose turn of phrase sometimes suffers from absorption with the business of communicating fact, were astonished that such vicious rioting was contained without a shot being fired by security forces throughout that day in Crater.

A few of my own recollections:

Lance-Corporal Robert Teit, aged nineteen, from Wallsend, doubles up in a shop doorway as smoke from a grenade clears. He gasps, 'It's nothing, man'. The blast winded him and he is wounded only in the elbow. A Geordie shout echoes down the narrow street, 'Movement right to left on rooftop – man in striped shirt'.

Soldiers kick open street doors to stairs and clamber like alpinists across steep roofs. Soon two terrified Arabs in Yemeni sarongs and turbans are bundled into Land-Rovers. One has a blue and white shirt. There is a smell of grease and powder on his palms. He is held on the floor with an army boot on his neck as the one soldier left to guard him warily scans the rooftops. Another Yemeni is brought from the house, prodded by gun butts and boots because he struggles while being searched. An officer intervenes: 'That's enough'.

All three prisoners are taken off for interrogation and likely detention for the remaining period of British rule, probably glad to be safely out of the inter-Arab battle, with a prospect should their own faction prevail of immediate release as a hero of the liberation the moment the British withdraw.

A corral of barbed wire coils set up on the parade ground inside the Arab Armed Police barracks begins to look like a wartime POW cage. Some twenty British families live in flats on the other side of the Queen Arwa road, directly overlooking the police barracks. Mrs Sheila Burlinge, from Todmorden, Lancashire, is alone with daughters aged three and seventeen months. There is only egg and chips for Sunday lunch because the little Arab shop near by where most family groceries are bought has been closed for four days, apart from furtive business under half-raised steel shutters as opportunity allows. Wives and children face the situation alone because husbands are on duty elsewhere.

(Soon afterwards, fortunately, in view of impending developments, all these families were moved to safer areas)

Next morning in front of the concrete latticework of the British Bank of the Middle East a decoy mob chants as they perform a whirling dervish dance behind banners and portraits of exiled leaders.

Fusiliers debouch from a Land-Rover and charge into them. The mob scatters, a shout of 'grenade' as a rifle barks, the dull boom of a grenade. Most of the patrol fling themselves to the ground in time, but through the smoke Fusilier William Davidge slumps against a wall and slides slowly down, finally rolling on one side along the pavement. He had stayed on his feet to shoot the grenadier, and been caught by shrapnel, but it turns out his wounds are not critical.

Across the road Corporal Harry Oliver holds a bloody knee with his left hand as he shouts 'Halt', first in English, then in Arabic, to a man running along a culvert. The man stops at the Arab command and raises his hands. More Arabs are rounded up. The tough young men of Tyneside are in ugly mood on this second day of the terrorist offensive. To understand just how they feel you need to be in Crater with them, not on the back benches of Parliament in Westminster. There's a lot of boot, gun butt and fist thumping. It isn't a display of brutality – it's a show of righteous human anger.

The British tried a change of tactics on Tuesday, Day Three of the 'Give the British hell' offensive.

The Northumberland Fusiliers stayed inside the police compound leaving the wild-eyed mobs to roam the maze of back alleys and bazaar squares, light bonfires and fight among themselves. The Arabs were jubilant. Mayor Fuad Khalifa, producing an airport tarmac pass as proof of identity, boasted to journalists that FLOSY was too strong for the British. Soon afterwards Haidar Shamshair, leader of a FLOSY commando, was riddled by bullets in an NLF ambush. His brother, Nassar, was shot in the eye and taken to hospital for treatment by British surgeons. FLOSY, characteristically, blamed the shooting on British-paid mercenaries.

That afternoon 1500 gathered for a FLOSY funeral in the Muslim cemetery. Twenty Arab commandos carried sten guns openly in the funeral procession. British troops kept out of sight, discreetly watching from rooftops through binoculars. But as the funeral ended two companies of Fusiliers, backed by armoured cars and tracked armoured troop carriers, set up a cordon between the cemetery and the town. Explained Lieutenant-Colonel Richard Blenkinsop, commanding the Fusiliers, 'They were welcome to burn down their town so far as I'm concerned, but we have to show them we can command the situation any time we choose.'

The mob ceased chanting as it came within sight of the line of young soldiers with white and red cockades in their berets, and tamely split into twos and threes to pass through the British line back to their homes. As the Muezzins called for sunset prayers silence descended over Crater.

The focus of interest switched back to the UN recluses in their seaside fastness. They had ignored three letters sent by the Federal Government suggesting courtesy calls on them. Two Aden politicians, also ministers in the Federal Government, petitioned to be heard as private individuals. A leader of the South Arabian League, the original nationalist party, asked to be allowed to give evidence. He was ignored too.

The members of the mission were not engrossed in reading paperback novels or watching home movies. They had sent a letter to Sir Richard Turnbull rejecting any kind of co-operation with the Federal authorities, asking for TV and radio time to broadcast a message to the people of South Arabia, and requested a visit to political detainees in Mansoura prison.

The prison visit was quickly set up. However, every prisoner refused to talk to them. There was a riot inside the prison while other terrorists opened fire with machine-guns and mortars on British security forces guarding the road approaches to the prison. Later Abdul Sattar Shalizi, from Afghanistan, was quoted as saying the British used the security situation as an excuse to keep them from meeting the local population. He particularly mentioned being taken by helicopter instead of by road on this prison visit. Journalists who had no alternative to road travel, and were kept waiting outside the prison perimeter, were fired on. A bullet buried itself in the metal of a white-coloured car driven by Nicholas Herbert of the London *Times* with whom I was riding.

The request for the TV address to the people had to be passed on by Government House to the Federal Government which controlled TV and radio stations. Despite the snubs it was agreed through British intermediaries for the Venezuelan member of the UN mission, Senor Manuel Perez-Guerrero, to make a statement on the Thursday evening. But when the Federal Information Minister, Hussein Ali Bayoumi, one of the Adenis whose application to talk to the mission as a private individual had been rejected, saw the videotape his mounting anger at the partisan attitude of the UN mission erupted.

As they sat expectantly around the TV set in the Seaview Hotel to watch the broadcast the men from the UN received a cumuppance for their rudeness to the *de facto* rulers of most of the area they seemed to assume was all under British rule. Instead of seeing Senor Perez-Guerrero they heard a brusque announcement that the broadcast would not take place, followed by the cold suggestion that the mission might make another application to use the facility directly to the Federal authority concerned.

The men from UNO angrily resolved to leave Aden to its fate, and phoned Government House demanding bookings on next day's flight to Rome. The UN Secretary-General, normally a consummate prevaricator, cabled an order for them to stay and complete their work. It was delivered as they were ready to leave Seaview by helicopter for the airport. They ignored it. It had been clear from the beginning that they had been unnerved by the noisy reception Aden's terror gangs had staged for their benefit. Junior members of the British High Commissioner's staff tabbed their visit 'Operation Chicken'. They were desperate to get out of the hellhole whose creation they and their kind had fostered regardless of the lives and security of countless innocent bystanders. They omitted all normal diplomatic courtesies before leaving for the airport.

Then came the final farce – the kind of incident not seen since the disaster of the UN peace-keeping intervention in the Congo. First the three men, presumably senior diplomats of their countries, engaged in an unseemly tarmac slanging match with the assembled world press. Then they refused crossly to submit their baggage to the RAF security searchers. Mali's Moussa Keita, wearing crocodile shoes and carrying a leopardskin briefcase, snarled, 'We are not terrorists'.

The press row flared when a British-born reporter from the Associated Press of America was told that the reason for their sudden departure was none of the world's business. The reporter retorted indignantly, 'Our readers have a right to know. Britain contributes a bloody sight more towards the United Nations than your countries'.

Dapper Abdul Satar Shalizi almost dropped his amber worry beads. He stammered, 'Your country contributes a bloody sight more bloodshed in the world than anybody else'.

An hour after the scheduled departure time the pilot of the BOAC VC-10, Captain Peter Fotherby, told the UNO men in blunt Yorkshire, 'I will not take you unless your bags are searched. Make up your minds now. We will delay no longer than a few more minutes'. Faced with being left standing on the tarmac of an airfield under constant threat of terrorist attack the UNO men decided to compromise. They agreed to BOAC crew members searching their baggage under RAF supervision.

A weary High Commission official watched the plane disappear northwards, and gave a deep sigh. He said, 'They came into a most bewildering situation, and were overwhelmed. A little flexibility on their part might have brought some progress. They could not grasp that we are not the colonial rulers of the whole area and merely in treaty relations with established regimes in the Federal states.'

The cable and telephone lines between London and Aden were busy as the curtain came down on this outrage against all the UN was founded to uphold. Political events followed swiftly. The Foreign Secretary, Mr George Brown, announced the appointment of Lord Shackleton as a sort of political supremo of the Aden withdrawal, and Sir Richard Turnbull left his flower beds at Steamer Point to the crows and Government House to a new and last British tenant.

Sir Humphrey Trevelyan, renowned trouble-shooting diplomat, veteran of Suez nationalization, revolutionary Iraq, Peking and Moscow, was brought out of retirement to be Britain's 'last viceroy' in a desperate eleventh-hour bid to salvage a fast-disintegrating situation.

12 Soldiers of the Sultans

Till well into 1967 Aden's 'little raj', holed up in its fortified compounds, retained a touching faith in the sense of duty of the Arab forces they were hastening to expand, train and equip to enable them to hold the ring for the emergence of representative government after the Union Jack was ceremonially lowered at a final handover ceremony at the end of the year.

Colonial officials waxed lyrical about these splendid desert warriors. It was hardly questioned that they would remain loyal to the hand that fed them. They had accepted British salt, so to speak, and that was a binding alliance among tribesmen. How we British cling to our myths! The British love affair with the desert Arab survived to the end in the environs of Government House in Aden. It is a most infectious beguiler. The Federal Army's praises were sung even by battalion and company commanders of British regular units.

Federal troops were only used within the boundaries of Aden colony to search mosques in liaison with British units. They carried out these duties with all the outward appearances of a soldierly manner.

The mosque searches mostly drew a blank despite certainty of British troops of their use by snipers and grenade throwers. A few FLOSY arms stores might occasionally be brought out along with suspects handed over to special branch interrogators, but nobody seemed to notice that no NLF terrorists were ever discovered in these raids on mosques.

The Arab township of Sheik Othman, just inside the flat desert borderlands with Lahej protectorate, was the scene of the first suburban set-piece gun battles with British troops. The huddle of palm thatch huts of the poor around modern high-rise apartments of the prospering brooded beside the only land route to Little Aden, and dominated the main road to Yemen.

The first time Federal soldiers were called into a joint operation on colonial territory in any strength was for an assault on Al Noor mosque dominating the main square of Sheik Othman. This white-walled venue for five-times-daily prayers was a known nest of NLF gunmen. Foot patrols of the first parachute battalion by-passed it. Armoured cars were often fired on by heavy machine-guns mounted in minarets at each corner. Under cover of these mosque guns terrorist strongholds were maintained in buildings all around it, threatening to make this key area of Sheik Othman a no-go area for British security forces.

Time-wasting political objections to the likely repercussions of cleaning out this terrorist lair were finally overcome, and the operation began with an attack by twelve armoured cars of the Queen's

Dragoon Guards on a blistering April day. The rule of minimum force forbade the use of seventy-six guns, the main armament of the armoured cars, but they poured withering heavy machine-gun fire into eight terrorist strongpoints in the vicinity of the mosque. Fire was returned from windows on every side. Bullets tore lines of washing on balconies, and pulverized wall plaster. Tracer from terrorist positions set ablaze the straw roof of a dairy, and cows and calves stampeded through the crossfire. Gunfire cut down the flag of the United Arab Republic raised high on a thin bamboo cane above the mosque.

Suddenly the gunfire slackened. I raised my head above a low wall, and saw army lorries crammed with turbaned Arab soldiers, speeding along the road leading to the mosque. The only sound was the singing of tyres on clammy hot tarmac as the guns on both sides fell silent. The lorries slithered to a halt close to a narrow alley that led to doorways into the mosque. Arab soldiers leapt out, in stocking feet, and charged into the mosque.

Gunfire started up again. First the tin can sound of Kalashnikovs from terrorist positions around the mosque; then the heavy clatter of heavier calibre fire as armoured cars moved up to fire into upper windows of surrounding buildings at closer range. The guns fell silent again as the Arab soldiers emerged from the mosque herding a frightened band of about fifty suspects.

General Sir John Willoughby, commanding all Aden security forces, asked an Arab captain whether any arms were found. The captain shook his head. The general grimaced, 'They must have been firing at us with catapults'.

To soften this biting sarcasm he turned to the British officer in command of the Federal force to add, 'Splendid show. Your chaps really looked like soldiers'. Snapped back Lieut-Colonel Richard Lawson, newly arrived on secondment to the Federal Army, 'They are soldiers'. Exemplary loyalty to his men in view of an incident on the mosque steps which came to my knowledge much later.

It had all looked highly impressive. There was as much noise of battle, as much dash and colour as a director of an old-style Hollywood spectacular could have wished for. Yet, so far as could be seen, not a drop of blood had been spilt. There were no casualties to the assault forces in their armoured vehicles, and nobody on the British side cared to investigate inside the buildings blasted by British fire.

It had looked strange to me at the time. It turned out there were no known terrorists among the prisoners, most of whom were released or ordered to be dumped on the Yemen frontier. Later I learned that Colonel Lawson had been prevented from entering the mosque by one of his own soldiers. He told me that a soldier in front of him stopped abruptly at the bottom of the steps leading to the mosque and thrust him back with his rifle muzzle. When he ordered the man to let him pass he was knocked to the ground. There was no question, apparently, of any disciplinary action being taken – a turning of a blind eye more in the tradition of Munich appeasement than a Nelson touch. British officers in the Arab army were having to behave like diplomats, not commanders of disciplined soldiers.

Britain was trying to replace the old treaty commitments to the traditional rulers with an immediate grant of £5 millions to the Arab armed forces to enable them to take over this protective role. This was to be followed by annual grants of £10.25 millions for three years after independence.

The existing five infantry battalions were to be increased to nine. A new artillery unit was to be trained in the use of twenty-five-pounders. Saladin armoured cars were delivered to a newly formed heavy armoured car unit. This crash reorganization raised the numerical strength of the Arab army by more than seventy per cent, and included replacement of obsolete rifles and three-inch mortars with up-to-date weapons including 84mm Karl Gustav anti-tank guns and 81mm mortars.

High priority was given to replacing the RAF's key role with a contract manned air force of armed BAC 167 jets, DC3 transports, Beavers and Sioux helicopters. Civilian pilots were recruited under contract through Airwork, Ltd., the British commercial company that recruits instructors for the Saudi Arabian air force.

The commander of this fast expanding Arab military force was Brigadier Jack Dye, who had commanded a battalion of British troops in the Radfan campaign of two years before. British personnel in June 1967 numbered about fifty officers and a hundred and fifty NCO technicians and instructors. It was planned that after independence a few army and navy technicians would also stay on as civilians under contract to the new authority. Three of the additional infantry battalions were formed by stiffening existing units of the Federal Guard, a tribal *gendarmerie*, with the more widely recruited regular units of the existing army. The ninth battalion was to be formed by recruitment with NCOs drafted from regular battalions.

The rush of volunteers for this expanded army was interpreted by most British officials, with forgiveable pride in smart parade ground discipline, as 'indicative of the high regard in which the force is held throughout the country'. Men from different tribes were drilling together in the same units in hopes of creating a new loyalty – to the idea of Federation before tribe, an inconceivable switch of loyalties in Arabia.

Basic rates of pay were enviable compared with other Arab armies, and matched good civilian wages. A captain received a basic £70 monthly, sergeant £23, corporal £21, private £18. Educational opportunities, medical services, accommodation and family welfare was on a par with British Army standards. Officers attended courses in Jordan as well as Camberley, Surrey.

Britons closest to the Arab army, the officers supervising this crash expansion, were becoming more and more apprehensive over the loyalty of their soldiers. The mutiny of a century before in India was an ever-present spectre, although the Arab police mutiny forty years before on Perim Island was either unknown or forgotten. These fears met with little sympathy from colleagues in British military headquarters, whose sleeping quarters were safely within the most secure areas of British control. Tough-mindedly, most resigned themselves fatalistically and learned to live in a state of constant wariness against treachery.

It had been hoped that recruits from the desert tribes would be uncontaminated by the seething politics of Aden's back streets. Since FLOSY was the faction with much larger original following in the urban area of Aden that was good thinking. The NLF was then a largely unknown factor in terms of leadership and following. But it was clear to British officers in the Arab army that loyalties were divided. The army was being drawn inevitably into the struggle for power raging around their camps.

The NLF was widely favoured in the army because unlike FLOSY it showed clear indications of determination not to take over power as mere puppets of President Nasser. FLOSY had a small following in the army along tribal lines.

Lessons learned in the Indian mutiny saved a bloody confrontation when Arab nationalist temper among the soldiers of the Federal Army first erupted. This was the practice of keeping personal weapons of native troops locked up, standard British

Army procedure since the Indian mutiny.

It was this precaution that thwarted Arab soldiers going on an angry rampage after a funeral one Saturday night in May 1967. Off-duty soldiers, who had been attending a hurriedly arranged funeral in civilian sarongs and shirts, surged back into barracks bent on obtaining weapons. The difficulty of access to them gave Arab officers a chance to calm them down. Earlier the bodies of a popular Arab colonel and two of his men, killed by a land mine on frontier patrol, had been brought back to Aden for burial. Because of climatic considerations the Kaid of the mosque ordered their burial before sunset, and the funeral was called at half an hour's notice.

Senior British officers, led by Admiral Sir Michael Le Fanu, the C-in-C, attended the service at a mosque in Lake Lines, the Federal Army cantonment near Khormaksar airport. So did relatives and friends of the dead men who came from different tribes. NLF banners were produced.

Representative mourners from the Royal Horse Guards, who had served under the dead Arab Colonel's orders, had to travel from their camp at Little Aden. They came by Land-Rover, and required an escort through the badlands around Sheik Othman, causing more delay while an escort was formed. By the time the Royal Horse Guards mourners, and escort, approached Lake Lines the funeral ceremony was over, and a procession was carrying the coffins from the mosque to the cemetery. But a wailing crowd, all in ordinary Arab civilian dress, screened the three coffins. All the approaching British soldiers could see was an Arab crowd and NLF banners. Armoured cars of the First Queen's Dragoons of the escort, with infantry of the Royal Anglians, deployed to face what appeared to them to be an illegal demonstration. As the soldiers checked their weapons there was a misfire over the heads of the chanting crowd of mourners. A uniformed National Guard among the mourners apparently fired a sten gun in panic. Three Federal soldiers fell wounded, spilling the open coffin they were helping carry. In the hysterical confusion that followed a group of Arab soldiers raced back to Lake Lines intent on obtaining their weapons and shooting it out with the infidel British.

While Arab officers sorted out the misunderstanding the entire British garrison stood to general alert. Troops were recalled from bars and restaurants. Europeans were warned to stay at home.

This sinister development, happily forestalled, was the first real warning of hair-trigger tensions in the generally trusted Arab forces. It was passed off with a bromide Aden Command statement that 'a dangerous situation between Federal soldiers was quickly brought under control by Arab officers'.

Plans had just been completed for the Federal Army to complete the takeover of the whole of the desert hinterland by 1 July, the oil refinery town of Little Aden by 1 October, and to move soon afterwards into Aden itself, district by district, as four rearguard British battalions withdrew one by one.

All this was happening when Aden's affairs passed almost unnoticed because of a sudden flare-up in the Arab-Israeli conflict, precipitated by a miscalculation by Nasser. As the Six Day War developed the Egyptian propaganda machine searched for a scapegoat for impending defeat, and Cairo's Voice of the Arabs radio screamed over the air waves the Big Lie of air intervention by British and American air forces. The wild voice from Cairo urged listeners throughout the Arab world: 'Kill the pirates and bloodsuckers'.

The scene was set for treachery and massacre, and a tawdry end to British rule in the old imperial fortress of Aden.

13 Mutiny and Massacre

Mutiny in the South Arabian armed forces flared murderously during the morning of Tuesday, 20 June 1967, the blackest day in Aden's history as a British colony. Before it was over twenty-three British soldiers – and a British civilian – were mown down by erstwhile Arab comrades in arms.

The first victims were men of the Royal Corps of Transport crowded into the back of a ten-ton lorry as it drove into a supply depot inside the security perimeters of the sprawling Khormaksar cantonment area. They were returning from a rifle practice range and had just uncocked their weapons on entering a 'protected area' as they came under withering fire from barrack huts of Arab soldiers in near-by Champion Lines. Eight were killed. So was a passing civilian employee of the Ministry of Works.

The Arab soldiers were shooting out of furious anger over the suspension of four colonels, notables of their tribes, for 'an act of gross indiscipline'. They had combined to petition the Federal Army Commander, Brigadier Jack Dye, and also the Federal Supreme Court, objecting to promotions of officers from the distant Aulaqi tribe believed to be less politically motivated than officers from some other tribes. First tribal factions in the army exchanged fire among themselves. Then a group of Federal Guards, a tribal force recently merged into the Federal Army, turned their guns on the first British targets that came within range.

Because of fears for British service families living near by the Federal Government was quickly persuaded to make a formal request for British troops to restore order in the Arab barrack huts at Champion Lines. A company of the King's Own Royal Border Regiment surrounded the barracks, suffering several wounded, in a decisive move backed by armoured cars of the Queen's Dragoon Guards. Loudspeakers announced that the colonels had apologized and been reinstated, and the entire misunderstanding would be overlooked if they put down their arms at once. The frightened Arabs surrendered, and were subsequently given a dressing down on the elements of soldierly behaviour and discipline by Brigadier Dye.

Meanwhile wild rumours of a big attack on the Arab army barracks by British soldiers, regarded as allies of Israel since Cairo's Big Lie, spread throughout Aden. It reached the one hundred and eighty men of the Arab Armed Police, a *gendarmerie* mainly recruited in the tribal areas, in their barracks in Crater. A routine patrol of the Northumberland Fusiliers, travelling in an armoured steel box on wheels called a 'pig', paused to push aside buses parked across the Queen Arwa dual carriageway, the main route between the only two passes into the mountain peak girdled district. They were unaware that the entire Aden garrison was on Red Alert because their radio was not working.

As they passed the Armed Police barracks further towards Main Pass they noted that a heavy machine-gun, a Bren, was positioned on the roof, and other defensive positions were manned. Two shots were fired after them as they reached the narrow opening between cliff faces at the top of Main Pass. The patrol commander, Second Lieutenant John Davis, decided to return to his company headquarters on Marine Drive to report these strange dispositions by the longer route through Khormaksar avoiding a return under the threatening guns of the Armed Police.

Red Alert was normally a signal for the Northumberland Fusiliers to move into Crater to set up temporary headquarters in the police barracks. It was a normal movement, made many times before in the year the battalion was responsible for Crater. Major John Moncur drove from company headquarters in Marine Drive to spearhead the battalion's move into an office and billets routinely set aside for this purpose in the Armed Police compound within a ten-foot stone wall that bordered the Queen Arwa Road. Behind him, in a second Land-Rover, was Major David Malcolm, liaison officer from the advance party of the Argyll and Sutherland Highlanders shortly relieving the Fusiliers for home leave. In the two vehicles there were six fusiliers and three Scots. As they slowed down to turn off the dual carriageway into a side road leading to the barrack gates, sudden withering fire caught them unawares.

It came from the Bren gun on the roof of the police barracks, from upper windows of flats on the opposite side of Queen Arwa Road and from over the wall of the police compound. The only survivor of the nine Britons in the Land-Rovers was Fusilier John Storey, then aged twenty. A few days later, sitting in hospital with three bullet wounds, he gave me the following account of the ambush:

'I was in the back of the second Land-Rover. Firing began as we came level with the Armed Police barracks. It was very heavy. The leading Land-Rover crashed against the wall of the barracks. We rammed the centre island of the dual carriageway and rolled out into the road.

'There was a hell of a lot of shooting and no cover at all. I tried to get as low as I could in the gutter beside the centre island. I saw the major firing from under the Land-Rover, but the vehicle was already beginning to burn. Just afterwards the major was lying still, and his batman lay in the road with his clothes on fire.

'I was hit in the back and the ribs, then in an arm. I thought I would be a gonner for sure if I stayed around . . .

'I made a run for it, zigzagging across the road to the doorway into a block of flats and ran up the stairs. There was nobody on the roof. All my mates seemed to be dead in the road below. Four of the bodies were burning. Shooting suddenly stopped.

'I tied a hanky around my arm to try to stop the bleeding.

Firing began again. There were two Arabs with guns on the next roof. I fired at them. One put his hands to his head and fell backwards. The other ran away.

'Then I found I was out of ammo. I had left my spare clip in the Land-Rover. You see, we hadn't been as alert as we would have been without the police barracks between us and the parts of Crater where sniper fire and grenades were normal.

'I went downstairs and saw a policeman across the road with a rifle. I thought they were still on our side and shouted to him, "John, come here". He raised his rifle and fired at me.

'I ran back upstairs and found an Arab at a third-floor doorway carrying a baby. I made him let me into his flat where women and children started screaming. I ordered them to the back of the flat and gathered all the men into the front-room overlooking the road. They didn't know I was out of ammo.

'Heavy machine-guns opened up outside and armoured cars went by at full speed. I thought the whole battalion would be coming soon.

'An Arab warned me that police had started searching the flats, so I ran downstairs and hid in an alcove. Then I found a window on to a side road. I pushed out my rifle and clambered out after it.

'Police spotted me and chased me. They soon caught me because of my injured leg. They put me into a three-tonner and drove into the barracks. Then they drove back to the dual carriageway where they piled the bodies of my mates into the truck with me as a crowd gathered around shouting for me to be killed.

'One man tried to make me say "Nasser tamam" – Nasser is best – but I just stared into space. Police and the crowd were shouting at each other. I think I was only saved by a new burst of firing that scattered the mob, and allowed the police to drive back to the barracks.

'The police were okay after that. An officer looked after me and gave me coffee and cigarettes. After about three hours an RAF ambulance with a British doctor and two medics, escorted by a police Land-Rover, arrived to collect me.'

The ambulance came under heavy fire itself from terrorist positions, who defied the truce agreed by telephone between the Aden Police Commissioner and the Chief Superintendent of the Armed Police, as it returned up the dual carriageway to Main Pass.

While Private Storey was in the flats, knowing all his companions were dead, Second-Lieutenant Davis had made his reports in person at company headquarters, and then followed his company commander into Crater from the Marine Drive entrance.

They saw the blazing Land-Rovers and bodies around them but heavy fire pinned them down by a garage at the end of the rows of high-rise flats. In the garage forecourt, covered by fire from an escorting Saracen armoured car, Davis and three riflemen left the shelter of the armoured 'pig', climbed a drainpipe to the roof of the flats and mounted a Bren gun hoping to give covering fire to any survivors of the ambush. Again Davis was dogged by an unserviceable radio. He ordered an Argyll liaison subaltern, accompanying the patrol in the 'pig', to return to Marine Drive to report the situation. Why the escorting Saracen was unable to do this has never been explained. The fate of the patrol has never been reliably explained either. All that is known is that they died that day. Rumours abound about how exactly they met their deaths.

Second-Lieutenant Nigel Stephens, of the Queen's Dragoon Guards, saw nothing of them when he drove through Queen Arwa Road later. He told me next day, 'Fire was so intense my Browning machine-gun was knocked out and I couldn't close the turret lid. Without cover from another Ferret we were pretty helpless. I asked permission to use my seventy-six to knock out the Bren gun position on the police roof, and waited while it was being cleared with the High Command. The answer was negative, and we were forced to retire even though we thought three British soldiers were alive in the near-by flats.'

Earlier the few British bank officials still bravely attending their desks in Crater were warned by telephone, and all slipped away through Marine Drive before roaming mobs took over Crater to celebrate the Arab repulse of the British Army. Frenzied mobs were known to make gory sport of three British soldiers, although it is not known whether any were still alive when captured. The bodies anyway were mutilated, kicked and dragged through the streets. Two were hanged in a macabre public trial and execution in the Maidan Square close by the police barracks. Mobs looted and burned the Legislative Council building, the original church before its conversion to political debate. A secondary school and bank offices were ransacked. The gates of the criminal jail, next door to the armed police barracks, were broken down and all the prisoners set loose. The Armed Police, frightened now of British retribution, opened the armoury and issued four hundred rifles to townspeople.

These were the police who had guarded the United Nations mission hotel just ten weeks earlier, and threatened to kill their British officer if he returned to duty supervising them there.

In the confusion terrorists had taken over an old Turkish fort dominating Main Pass and were firing down on the main road below. This was the only land link between the British command and commercial district of Steamer Point and the airport at Khormaksar.

The deeply worried civil and military leaders in Government House and on Flagstaff Hill refused to be hustled. They had to stifle warm-blooded emotions and coolly consider wider implications. Foremost in these considerations was the likely fate of hundreds of Britons trapped in remote desert locations whose fate might well be sealed by any further extension of disaffection in the Arab security forces. It was desperately necessary to play at least for time until they could be pulled back into the safety of fortress Aden. Orders went out immediately for all British officials and personnel to abandon up-country posts, and the last British units were pulled out of road building and other up-country duties.

Because of this the immediate British response was limited to sealing off the rebellion in Crater, an apparent timidity deeply resented by the comrades in the battalions of the men murdered. Containment of the insurrection within Crater necessitated a limited counter-attack to recapture control of Main Pass and the strategic peaks along the rocky rim around Crater. Royal Marine commandos, reinforced by grimly angry Fusiliers, stormed the heights above Main Pass on the second day of the Crater rebellion. They used ladders to scale sheer cliffs, and establish a line of picquet posts along the ridges of Mount Shamshan.

The old Turkish fort dominating Main Pass held out against heavy machine-guns, the most powerful weapon the assault troops were allowed to use under their own doctrine of minimum force. The battle was suspended for an hour while permission was sought for use of the 120-pounder of a Saracen armoured car. As they waited the soldiers, smarting under heavy casualties and stories of the mutilation of dead comrades, were scathingly critical of what they believed was an excessively soft-glove attitude by the high command. When permission came it was conditional on only one round being fired.

Greatest care was taken to ensure it was smack on target, but when the order came to fire it – nothing happened. The precious round, kept so long as an ultimate deterrent, had become a dud. Officers on the spot decided it didn't count, and a second shell was locked into the breach. This time all went well – except for the terrorists blown up as it slammed into the fort.

Later that night ten bodies of soldiers killed in the previous day's ambush were delivered to a British picquet on Marine Drive by a group of the Arab Armed Police. This was arranged during efforts by Aden Colony's Police Commissioner, Peter Owen, to persuade his men to end the mutiny. He was in constant telephone contact with their Arab commander at Crater barracks, Chief Superintendent Mohamed Ibrahim, pressing arguments for a return to police duties and aloofness from politics while the misunderstanding was sorted out.

This attitude of appeasement won time for Britons in vulnerable places to be called back to safer areas. It also emboldened the Arabs of Crater. They quickly set aside fears of a crushing show of British force descending upon Crater to exact an awesome vengeance for the high toll of British dead. On the third day loudspeakers from Aidrus Mosque, notorious nest of grenade throwers and snipers, blared the announcement that the 80,000 residents of Crater were now liberated from colonialism and under 'nationalist control', that the British had been expelled for all time, and that Crater's independence would soon be shared by other districts of Aden.

Both carriageways of the Queen Arwa Road were closed by deep-parked buses and lorries, one obstruction at the lower end, the other above the police barracks. A blue police flag hung limply over the Armed Police barracks which appeared to be deserted. Men in British observation posts logged every significant movement in the close-packed streets that lay below them like a mock-up model. Police Commissioner Owen had instructed his deputy, Mohamed Ibrahim, to hold an official inquiry into the 'misunderstanding' of 20 June. Its outcome appears to have been 'lost' in the archives.

No community could have been more easily starved into submission than Crater's. The idea was immediately ruled out because of the suffering it would cause to the innocent majority in an area where Aden's oldest families lived. This had already weighed heavily as a factor against a crushing counter attack on the mutinous police. The military command, shocked at the firepower held by the rebels, had demanded waiving of political restrictions on heavy armament as an only alternative to unacceptably heavy British casualties.

The British lines at both road entrances to Crater took on the look of a customs post on a Cold War frontier. Streams of people walked out. They were made to submit to a body search and every article carried was examined by brusque soldiers of the Argylls. Cars were also allowed through after thorough searches. Herds of goats passed into Crater destined for the empty slabs of butcher shops. Lorries of vegetables and fruit followed. By nightfall there was busy two-way traffic as Crater residents even took an evening drive to cool off.

Outside Crater commercial firms were running out of cash because the colony's currency reserves were locked up in the vaults of the Crater head offices of all the banks.

Meanwhile gunmen of the NLF and FLOSY began a savage civil war in the back alleys of Crater township – a somewhat unequal struggle since the mutinous armed police favoured the NLF. For all that the first notable casualty was the NLF's military commander in Crater, Abdul Bani Makrum Audhali, shot dead by one of the convicts released when the mob broke open the jail.

Three nights later NLF gunmen kidnapped the FLOSY chief of military operations, Fuad Khalifa, from a coffee shop. Khalifa doubled as Mayor of Aden municipality and senior executive of Aden Airways. His uncle had thrown Aden's first terrorist grenade – as the then Governor and senior British officials boarded a plane for London in December 1963.

Occasionally British snipers intervened in the factional gun battles. They kept constant vigil through telescopic rifle sights, itching for targets of opportunity fitting the rules of play laid down by the British High Command. With cold neutrality they picked off any civilian carrying a gun whether he might belong to the NLF or FLOSY. In ten days the kill reached ten, one terrorist for each British soldier killed within Crater on the day of the mutiny. The police barracks was specifically laid down as a non-firing zone. One marine commando sniper, a twenty-four-year-old from Northants, clearly relished the task. He told me, 'I saw an Arab carrying an SLR rifle that could only have been captured in last week's ambush of the Fusiliers. I felt good when I saw him fall to my shot.'

By this time the Federal rulers had become deeply worried that an independent Crater might be given formal recognition as the capital of a new state by the revolutionary Arab governments. They sent a delegation to Sir Humphrey Trevelyan suggesting that the Federal Army should reimpose governmental authority in Crater, making it known that British troops would not be returning.

Britain's High Commissioner rejected this offer, and made it clear that Britain's authority would be restored in Crater before final independence. He was able to speak more firmly because no Britons remained in high danger outside British perimeters.

Arab gunmen succeeded in shooting down a helicopter ferrying water, supplies and reliefs to picquets commanding the heights around Crater. The pilot, Sergeant Martin Forde, managed to keep the falling aircraft upright despite a bullet in his knee. The machine slithered down a slope and came to rest at the bottom. One passenger, a corporal, was thrown clear and badly hurt in the fall. The second, Fusilier John Duffy, on his way home to Britain after his last turn of duty on Temple Hill, a redoubt inside Crater's rim, dragged the wounded pilot clear and salvaged the radio before the helicopter burst into flames. He made a radio SOS, attended the two wounded men, and prepared to fight off any Arabs who might approach. All three were safely picked up by a Medivac helicopter within fifteen minutes. This was a fittingly heroic footnote to the Northumberland Fusiliers' one-year tour of duty in Crater, where they had controlled Aden's most turbulent area without one fatal injury to themselves until the Armed Police treachery.

There was one last parade for these bitter young men from Britain before they flew away from Aden at the end of a tough year of service. Twenty-five miles from Crater in a stark stretch of desert called Silent Valley they gathered to bury those whose families in Britain were never to see them again.

An 8 a.m. sun hung over the British Military Cemetery near Little Aden like a pale white moon through the heat haze. A Union Jack hung limply in the still air half way down its pole. Long rows of open graves stretched level with the parade shine of boots. Plain teak coffins with the remains of twenty-five men killed five days before had already been lowered into them. At the head of each grave lay the Union Jack that had covered a coffin earlier, clusters of poppies, and a teak wooden cross embossed with a name, rank, unit, date of birth and the date they all died – 20.6.67. Nearly all were born between 1943 and 1949, most were war demob babies.

Beside each grave stood a single soldier from the dead man's unit, tight-lipped, square-jawed, straining to keep themselves under emotional control. Tears mingled with the sweat running down cheeks of older, hardened soldiers.

A grey-haired man in a dark suit and tie stood incongruously among the soldier sentinels. He stood beside the grave of a Ministry of Works colleague, the only civilian victim of the mutiny, Hugh Alexander, aged thirty-four, from Kirkcudbrightshire. His widow sat among service wives. Their eight-year-old son and five-year-old daughter were left with family friends in Aden.

Sir Humphrey Trevelyan, representing the Queen, his gnomish head bowed, furrowed brow crowning a face that lacked its usual sardonic smile, experiencing a rare glimpse of the realities behind the paper reports, the conferences where decisions were never clouded by too close a view of events.

Five padres of different denominations shared the brief committal service as armoured cars patrolled the desert and helicopters hovered overhead. There was no address, for none but bitter words were felt – only a simple reading of 'The Lord is My Shepherd'.

Irish Guardsmen fired three volleys in salute. A single Scots piper played a lament. A bugler sounded the 'Last Post'.

Nobody knew it at the time, but this was to be the last full scale ceremonial parade in British Aden.

14 Mad Mitch and the Argylls

On the day of the mass funeral a lone Briton went back into Crater, the first to show a white face there since the massacre. Police Commissioner Peter Owen went to assure a hundred and eighty men of the Arab Armed Police that there would be no retribution for the killing of the British soldiers ... if they returned to duty and helped re-establish law and order.

Later that evening Commissioner Owen told me that the police
had fired on the troops in panic. They had been told that British
troops had attacked an armed police barracks in Khormaksar
and were about to launch an attack on them. He said the police in
Crater were now standing aloof from exchanges of fire between
Arab gunmen and British snipers, but were under the orders of
Arab officers and carrying out routine duties as normally as
possible. They had resumed guarding banks and preventing
looting. They had rearrested eleven of two hundred and fifteen
convicts released from jail, and collected back three hundred and
ninety-nine of four hundred rifles handed out in the panic of the
previous Tuesday.

Mr Owen spent two hours in Crater. 'I walked around, waved
and chatted to people,' he said. 'They were surprised to see me.
Some cheered and clapped. None were sullen.'

He added, 'I addressed the Armed Police in their barracks and
the Aden State Police (who did not join the mutiny) at their
station. I told them their duty was to be above politics and
maintain law and order. Everybody I spoke with was opposed to the
return of British troops, not only the police. All said it was the
presence of British troops that caused most trouble.'

'What now?' I asked.

'Back to normal terrorism . . . the police can do little about that
in these closing days of British rule.'

This courageous visit – appeasing as it so clearly was – brought
a quick positive result. The Armed Police put a cordon around the
Chartered Bank, opposite the ruins of the Legislative Assembly,
while Commissioner Owen and two British bank officials supervised
the removal of fifty cases of South Arabian currency notes (worth
£4 millions) in a convoy of seven green Federal Government
Land-Rovers from vaults that had withstood mob ransacking.
This allowed banks outside Crater to open doors for business
again for the first time in a week. Another £15 million worth of
gold and currency was left in the vault under Arab Armed Police
guard.

Life in liberated Crater was fraught by fear of rival terrorist
gangs, each trying to wipe out the other and intimidate the ordinary
population. More than six hundred and fifty Crater residents left
by car, by bicycle and on foot for other districts. Children left
their homes carrying household goods and helping shepherd
goats and poultry, passing through the British cordon like refugee

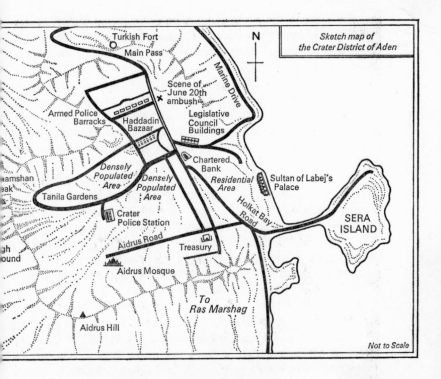

Sketch map of
the Crater District of Aden

Turkish Fort

Main Pass

N

Scene of
June 20th
ambush

×

Marine Drive

Armed Police
Barracks

Haddadin
Bazaar

Legislative
Council
Buildings

Chartered
Bank

Densely
Populated
Area

Densely
Populated
Area

amshan
eak

Tanila Gardens

Residential
Area

Sultan of Labej's
Palace

Holkat Bay Road

SERA
ISLAND

Crater
Police Station

gh
ound

Aidrus Road

Treasury

Aidrus Mosque

To
Ras Marshag

Aidrus Hill

Not to Scale

columns so familiar wherever order breaks down.

The accepted military assessment was that it would require a major military operation to reoccupy Crater, and cause a blood-bath. But a cocky little battalion commander of the Argyll and Sutherland Highlanders named Lieutenant-Colonel Colin Mitchell, son of a Croydon solicitor, confidently put in a formal request to military chiefs on Flagstaff Hill for his Highlanders to re-enter their full area of responsibility. Colonel Mitchell asserted that he could make Arabs swallow the triumphant taunts at British humiliation so much resented by his troops while avoiding heavy loss of life.

His soldiers knew every street in Crater although none had so far put a foot inside it. Back at barracks in Plymouth, Colonel Mitchell had mocked up the Crater lay-out and built models so that its landmarks were familiar tactical positions fitting into a familiar pattern of streets and buildings. For realism the battalion gymnasium at Plymouth had been superheated.

While the Arabs in Crater became more and more complacent

and the Voice of the Arabs radio from Cairo jeered nightly at the frailty of the toothless British Lion, official spokesmen put it about that the British were likely to leave Crater to its premature independence. The bland suggestion was that its recapture was just not worth any further loss of British or innocent Arab lives. Throughout the Middle East people believed tall stories of Arab victories regardless of facts, so prestige was not a valid enough reason. Why not, indeed, leave Crater and its troublesome population isolated for the remaining months of British responsibility for Aden?

Meanwhile the Argylls manning road blocks on Main Pass and the shore road from Khormaksar, frontiers of British control, became increasingly angry with the military command and Government House for meek acceptance of humiliation.

Morale suddenly lifted. Patrols in stocking feet, faces blackened, began slipping into Crater at night pinpointing Arab positions. SAS patrols from surrounding peaks confirmed that Arabs were relaxed, even off guard, at night.

As the huge red ball of the sun dropped into the ocean beyond the eternal flame from the Little Aden refinery on 3 July I met an officer of Colonel Mitchell's staff as I was leaving the Crescent Hotel in Steamer Point. 'I can't say more than advise you to follow me if you want a good story,' he said enigmatically. He led the way through Maalla's 'bloody mile' of straight dual carriageway, left the steep twisting road to Main Pass on our right, and skirted Crater's inland ridges to reach the Khormaksar beach on the other side of the peninsula. We had no doubt what was about to occur. It was already dusk when we reached the Argylls' road block on the shore road which marked the end of British control.

Colonel Mitchell stood beside his command Land-Rover in ebullient mood. He almost crooned the news, 'My Jocks are going in.' Through the gathering gloom we could see soldiers in their jaunty glengarries with distinctive red and white dicing and black ribbons hanging down to the back collar, waiting beneath the rock faces, bandoliers with one hundred rounds for each man slung around their waists and shoulders. They were laughing, eager, sure of success, hiding such fears as they felt beneath the general esprit de corps.

'The operation is code-named Stirling Castle after our regimental headquarters in Scotland,' said the colonel, opening a briefing around the bonnet of his Land-Rover.

His objective, he explained, was limited to control of the area around the Chartered Bank, tallest building in the commercial core of Crater, commanding its key road junction at the lower end of the infamous Queen Arwa dual carriageway. This would avoid any close approach to the Arab Armed Police barracks half-way up the dual carriageway towards Main Pass.

Anticipating the question he went on, 'I am authorized to use .76 guns in supporting armoured cars if necessary. If we need this main armament I shall not hesitate to use it . . . I won't be in the position my three chaps were put in with the Northumberland Fusiliers.' This was, in fact, the first time discretion was delegated below Command level for use of weapons heavier than machine-guns.

Suddenly the sweltering night was a skirl of wheezing noise. Pipe Major Kenneth Robson was marching up and down beside a file of men from 'B' company whose relaxed banter froze into tight lipped expectation. The sound of the pipes was joined by the rattle of heavy machine-guns in a routine dusk exchange of fire with Arab positions on Sira Island just off Crater's shingle beach.

The colonel said, 'We've been entertaining them with pipes and bang-bang for several nights. It's become routine dusk procedure. Tonight we shall surprise them with a bigger show.'

The pipes changed their tune from 'Campbeltown Loch' to 'Monymusk', the regimental charge. 'B' company moved off silently in single column through the intense darkness that follows a brief tropical dusk. Colonel Mitchell was in radio chat with other units also on the move. The pipes played a different tune. Colonel Mitchell laughed, 'The words of this one go "If I were a whisky I'd drink you dry".'

Then we set off behind 'B' company towards Crater, hugging the shelter of garden walls along villas below sheer cliffs and the beach. Bullets pinged off rock faces. Tracers poured into houses along the Esplanade. Flashes lit up rooms in an eerie pink glow. Soon the firing slackened to odd bouts of sniping. Somewhere up ahead Major Patrick Palmer came on the walkie-talkie link to ask permission to fire on a gun position in the shoreside palace of the Sultan of Lahej. Colonel Mitchell asked, 'Where will fire fall beyond?'

'Possibly around a block of flats.'

'Then don't fire at that angle,' the order went back.

The burnt-out shell of a school loomed through shadows on the

left, then the ruins of the Legislative Council building, a former
church, were etched against the night sky on a rocky escarpment
on our right. The corner of the Chartered Bank jutted out like a
ship's prow into the junction facing up Queen Arwa Road, a deadly
place to be caught in a crossfire from many points overlooking it.
The doors into the building were around that corner.

Colonel Mitchell pondered whether to blow a hole in the bank
wall. 'I've never broken into a bank before,' he whispered. It was
all still now, and suddenly quiet. It had to be a trap. A flare fired
from the area of the police barracks lit up the scene around us,
but no scything hail of bullets came out of the surrounding darkness. As the flare sputtered out the Scots battered in the back door
of the bank, and the main objective of the attack was in their
hands.

Armoured cars came up, swung around that exposed corner
and raced along the Esplanade and along the Causeway to link
with units landed by helicopter. The gun positions on Sira Island
were silenced. Three-tonner lorries began unloading pre-filled
sandbags and oil drums, raw material of new road blocks and
strongpoints.

Colonel Mitchell established a temporary command post on the
terrace of the Aden Commercial Institute below a tablet com-
memorating its opening by Governor Tom Hickenbotham in
1952. By this time the battalion had fanned out through the
commercial area and occupied all the banks. Arab Armed Police
guarding Grindleys, where the £15 million currency reserve was
locked in vaults, were persuaded to co-operate by Arabic-speaking
Major Nigel Crowe who had once served in the Federal Army. The
battalion had moved far beyond the limited objectives of this smooth
takeover. Their observation posts overlooked the market square
in the heart of Crater. They overran the hilltop headquarters of
the Aden Colony police, the ordinary 'beat' policemen who had
taken no part in the mutiny. Grinned Colonel Mitchell, 'I like
to get way ahead of the objective I've been ordered to take.'

Through the rest of the night there was no more than desultory
gunfire. One burst came from the police barracks. Scottish soldiers,
now established in rooftop observation posts overlooking it,
reported that the shooting came from two cars careering out
of the gates. This was believed to indicate a breakdown in relations
between the mutinous police and terrorist gunmen.

Crater's residents were left in no doubt about who had become overnight boss of Crater. The battalion's twelve pipes and four drums greeted the 5.30 a.m. sunrise with what Scots call a 'Long Reveille', fifteen ear-splitting minutes of it, including a number called 'Hey Johnny Cope' that harks back to the Forty-five Rebellion when Scottish rebels taunted a redcoat English colonel. It was an excruciating dawn after such a night.

Later that first morning Colonel Mitchell won the 'Mad Mitch' nickname that made him famous when he took my photographer colleague, Terry Fincher, and myself on a hair-raising guided tour of the worst areas of Crater, still far from secure against grenades and sniping. He left his usual bodyguard in the Land-Rover at one point to swagger through the market stalls and along narrow alleys greeting Arabs with smiles and handshakes. Gunmen must have been too stunned to react quickly to such a tempting target of opportunity.

Colonel Mitchell's flare for publicity was already bringing private brickbats along with public plaudits for the manner of his re-capture of Aden, achieved without a single British casualty and the known deaths of only two Arabs, both gunmen. His officers and men would hear no slight against him. A 'Sassenach' officer in one of the armoured cars attached to his command told me, 'His clowning is a bit hard to take, but I'd follow him anywhere.'

The Colonel's pride in his regiment was near pathological, perhaps because he was born in Croydon, son of a solicitor wounded and decorated as an officer of the Argylls in World War One. Incidentally, the Colonel's wife was a niece of the composer of 'The Dashing White Sergeant'.

Colonel Mitchell began soldiering at the age of fourteen as, perhaps, Britain's youngest Home Guard. He fought as a subaltern in the Argylls on the River Po front in the last year of World War Two. He was wounded fighting Jewish terrorist gangs in Palestine, fought in the Korean War. Then came service in Cyprus, where a son was born; Kenya, where a second son was born; Borneo, while his daughter was born in Singapore; ending his military career in triumph and controversy in Aden. He summed up his own assessment of British policies in Aden as 'old English humbug'.

The Argylls' spectacular triumph thrilled Britain in a jingoistic way reminiscent of such old-time imperial successes as the relief of Mafeking. But in Aden, itself, there was a tendency to hate the guts of the perky battalion commander who had made himself a national hero overnight.

Major-General Philip Tower, the General-Officer Commanding, had limited the first phase to a four-hundred-yards advance along Marine Drive, a mere nibble at Crater.

He was away at a dinner party in Little Aden when his deputy, Brigadier Charles Dunbar, agreed to the case Colonel Mitchell made for at least a bite at the real objective. He was given the okay to take about one-quarter of the area, the lower part of the township where all the banks were situated. During the course of the operation Brigadier Dunbar had also assented to the further advance that made the Argylls master of fully half the township in one night.

Major General Tower visited Colonel Mitchell's command post, labelled 'Stirling Castle' in huge letters across the front of the Commercial Institute, and spent ten minutes alone with him. He said afterwards, 'Last night's operations secured Crater at the cost of two Arab lives. It was a very skilled, highly professional operation.'

Months later when it was all over spiteful men in high places saw to it that Colonel Mitchell's cocky presumption had its come-uppance. Colonel Mitchell was awarded a mere 'mention in despatches' – a shabby reaction to his showman's flare by which the entire battalion was less than worthily honoured. However, it was this battle honour that undoubtedly swung the decision to maintain the Argyll name when other famous infantry regiments were faded out in a later reorganization of the army.

The support squadron of the Queen's Own Dragoons paid a tasteful tribute to the Northumberland Fusiliers, with whom they had previously operated in Crater, by carrying the red and white hackles of the Geordies on their radio masts. The Fusiliers were by that time back in Britain.

Just up the dual carriageway the mutinous Arab Armed Police brooded in their barracks. General Tower had ordered that they must be left strictly alone. 'We don't want to start any sparks,' he explained. There were now justified fears that the nine battalions of the Federal Army would turn their new equipment against British troops if it came to a showdown with the police mutineers. The Arab army was showing clear signs of breaking up into support of the rival nationalist factions.

At hilltop Central Police Division headquarters – ordinary colonial police – the Arab constables seemed friendly, though clearly apprehensive as they watched the Argylls strengthening barricades around the building. Superintendent Mohamed Ayash, the Somali officer-in-charge, told me, 'This is a very sad day. We are sorry to see the British soldiers back. We had told the people that they would not be coming back to Crater. The morale of my men has nose-dived. I expect trouble from them as well as from the population.'

That afternoon the police quit the police station area, leaving it to the Argylls to face sniping from near-by rooftops.

About the same time Chief Superintendent Mohamed Ibrahim, commander of the Armed Police barracks, called at the 'Stirling Castle' command post. Colonel Mitchell warned him that if he had any trouble he was prepared to wipe out the Arab Armed Police to the last man. He explained that his men were fresh from bloody fighting in Indonesia – that they were hillmen, like the Armed Police, and believed in deeds, not words. A quaking police chief was made to assent to two necessary guarantees before the Scots soldiers could be expected to work with the police again. These were the handing over of those responsible for the 20 June ambush for trial by the civil authorities, and police action to clear terrorists from rooftops overlooking the dual carriageway.

This grim-faced, hard-toned meeting was followed by talks between the Arab police chief and General Tower at 'Stirling Castle' next day. High Commissioner Sir Humphrey Trevelyan, escorted by a troop of armoured cars, looked in at the opening of the talks. He paused afterwards to congratulate 'all troops who have taken part in a very successful operation'. The only un-diplomatic touch was an aroma of frying pork chops – anathema to Muslims – which drifted into the conference room from a field kitchen in the courtyard.

After ninety minutes General Tower saw the police chief off, and blandly announced to waiting correspondents, 'We shall be back to a working relationship. There is no question of recrimina-tions.'

Soon afterwards Scots soldiers cleared the debris of the two Land-Rovers destroyed in the ambush, opening the road between Crater and the rest of Aden via the direct Main Pass route. Before dusk traffic was flowing as though nothing had happened. Crater passed a peaceful night.

The policy of forgiving conciliation was carried to extremes of cynical hypocrisy on the third day of renewed British control in

Crater. General Tower took the salute at a ceremonial march-past of the Arab Armed Police on their barracks square. On the surface this charade was a splendid colonial occasion. A crumpled Union Jack hung limply from a flagpole. But bitter distrust soured the still, humid atmosphere. Arab and British eyes were equally wary. Trigger fingers were tense. Guns of British armoured cars and rifles of the Scots soldiers covered every rooftop around. Police sepoys in flared scarlet turbans, officers with flashing swords at the salute, wore scowls on their tight-lipped faces.

General Tower carried it off with the smooth aplomb becoming a former director of Army public relations. He managed to conceal whatever discomfort he felt at returning the salute of a parade of men responsible for the treacherous murders beyond the boundary wall just seventeen days earlier. Major David Malcolm, one of the Argyll victims, had been a star cadet during the general's time as commandant at Sandhurst. In staging this public rehabilitation of the Arab Armed Police the general saw his duty as safeguarding the lives of his soldiers since they had no cause but a lost one, and was ready to swallow a lot to cool the situation. Neither Sir Humphrey Trevelyan, nor the Commander-in-Chief Admiral Sir Michael Le Fanu, were advised that the parade was being held. Neither was the combined forces press office. All heard of it with shocked disapproval.

Officers of the Argylls, headed by the imperturbable Colonel Mitchell, stood behind the general, dour faced as the police pipe and drum band – a still-surviving legacy of British cultural imperialism around the world – played 'Scotland the Brave'. All wore kilts on Colonel Mitchell's orders so that battalion riflemen surrounding the area might more easily tell friend from foe in the event of renewed treachery. Major Ian Mackay, who took over the vacant command of 'D' company, carried his dead predecessor's crummock – a crook-like walking staff.

It was this same parade ground that the Northumberland Fusiliers – whose X company suffered nine dead in the June Twenty massacre – used as a bivouac during their rumbustious spells of Crater duty, conducted more in textbook terms of internal security assistance to the civil authority than as an iron occupation force.

On a wooden support of the veranda close to the spot where General Tower stood at the salute someone had cut the tragic epitaph of the Geordies.

It read: 1 RNF
          X Coy
          Days to go:

Beneath it was several rows of notches with all but the last three cancelled out.

This stomach-retching policy of appeasement was justified to the extent that it worked. Crater, dominated by its no-nonsense Scottish chieftain from permanent headquarters in the strategically placed Chartered Bank building, became the most peaceful part of Aden. For the next eight days, while gun battles, grenade attacks, murders raged on in every other district there was not one incident in Crater.

Then two Argylls were wounded by a grenade tossed at a working party erecting a wire perimeter around their quarters in a boys' school. It looked like an isolated incident. Three more days passed peacefully as the Argylls held the district under close watch from an interlocked system of observation posts and roadblocks throughout Crater. Then five soldiers were wounded in two simultaneous grenade attacks.

The firm courtesy the Argylls had been showing in policing the area was replaced with iron measures. An Arab was shot dead running away after an order to halt. Several hundred were rounded up and kept in unshaded wire cages through the afternoon heat before being screened and released. Phone lines from Crater to Government House and military headquarters at Steamer Point were jammed with complaints from irate citizens. The Arab Armed Police were huffed because it was all done without their co-operation.

Colonel Mitchell's response was terse. 'We don't like having hand grenades thrown our way, and we intend to make our displeasure clear to Crater people.'

The NLF was regaining some confidence after the shattering swiftness of the recapture of Crater and the firm domination of the Scots over every corner of it. The only no-go areas were the township's fifteen mosques. A pattern of incidents showed that every grenade attack was made within a few yards' running distance of a mosque. With the aid of Japanese binoculars bought from a duty-free shop (£80 each from battalion welfare funds) the mosques were kept under almost microscopic observation. On a late July day a young Scot tensed as he saw three Arabs leave the Mahdani

L.S.–H

mosque two hundred yards below his observation post. One was carrying a Russian FI grenade openly in his right hand. Before the soldier could exchange the binoculars for his rifle the Arabs passed out of sight down the street.

He described it to me later in the day: 'About thirty seconds after they left the mosque I heard the boom of a grenade so I waited with my rifle lined up on the mosque doorway. Within a few seconds the same three men, all in white shirts, two in blue sarongs, one in a brown sarong, reached the open double doors of the mosque together. I fired two shots and all three slumped in the doorway. It all happened too quickly for me to see whether one was being helped along by the other two.'

At first it was thought all three had been killed by two shots. But doctors discovered that two died from bullet wounds in the head and one from multiple grenade splinters, indicating that the grenade had gone off prematurely.

In no-quarter exchanges over following weeks the Argylls lost four men killed, six wounded. In the same period nine Arab terrorists were shot dead, and it was confidently expected to take this figure to at least twelve – one for each British soldier killed in the massacre – before the district was handed over to the Federal Army as the Argylls pulled back into a tightening British perimeter around the airport and Steamer Point.

This rough justice had the effect of making Crater, so long the worst hotbed of trouble, a no-go area for terrorists. The Arabs showed respect for the authority of the gun when wielded ruthlessly without normal squeamish British constraint. The Scots never troubled to hide their preference for a terrorist shot dead over a cringing prisoner destined for a few weeks in Al Mansour jail with a TV set, and ultimate release as a hero of a revolutionary war. For almost three months Crater was an oasis of peace – forty-two straight days without a single incident in August and September – as Arabs fought a bloody civil war all around it.

In October there was a midday raid on the South Arabian Treasury. Fifteen masked men stole £20,000 in sacks of notes as it was being transferred to the vaults of the National and Grindlay Bank's main branch in the same building. They came through a vulnerable back door out of sight of an Argyll observation post that covered the front. To do so they pushed aside workmen fitting a new internal steel door to prevent access from the back of the building.

Little over a week later, perhaps emboldened by that success, an attack was made on Colonel Mitchell himself. It came late in the evening of 7 November, a day when NLF flags were flying everywhere else in Aden, and Arabs brandishing Kalashnikovs and hand grenades were touring the main streets of Maalla and Steamer Point, still nominally under British control, in triumph – tolerantly waved through what purported to be British army checkpoints. Only Crater was isolated from this euphoria that erupted with news that the British were ready to talk with the NLF. In Crater an Arab carrying a gun or grenade was certain to be shot on sight.

The grenade was tossed from behind the high wall around the Armed Police barracks close by the scene of the June massacre. Colonel Mitchell emerged from the smoke unscathed but three of his escorts were slightly wounded.

Within twelve hours the Argylls exacted a macabre revenge – a 'bag' as they put it of five dead Arabs. 'We got a couple of brace,' said a wickedly grinning lieutenant as he took me down to the vaults of the Chartered Bank used as a trophy room cum morgue. The grotesque bodies of four fat Arabs, one of whom I recognized as a taxi driver I had ridden with often, were piled on a bench like so many carcases. A fifth Arab was shot later running away after a challenge.

The four in the vault were members of an NLF kidnap gang. They had opened fire with a pistol when their two taxis were halted at a roadblock. Three other NLF men were captured and handed over to the Arab police. Their victim, a FLOSY man, was released to return to a refuge of frightened FLOSY survivors, holed up in a narrow alley ending in a sheer rock face, safe from liquidation only by the presence of the Scots.

Peace, thus firmly imposed, stayed in Crater until the Argylls left as suddenly as they arrived during the night of 25 November.

15 On Active Service

While happenings in Crater spotlighted the tragic finale to the role of the Northumberland Fusiliers and the hard-fisted triumphs of the Argylls, thousands of other British soldiers were also in hot combat. Terrorists mounted a maximum effort in other parts of Aden to offset their defeat in Crater.

The front line with a hostile Arab world was in desert saltpans around the notorious Arab township of Sheik Othman. There the soldiers' role was mainly to sit and take attacks by anti-tank rockets. These made movement hazardous even for those riding in bullet-proof Saladin armoured cars. This area of fighting, more akin to a set-piece battle than internal security, was shared by the Lancashire Regiment and the First Parachute Regiment.

The most forward observation post was beside the main road on the colonial boundary between Aden and the protected state of Lahej. It overlooked the main street of Dar Saad, a rest and resupply centre for terrorist gunmen.

Most Arabs in Dar Saad carried weapons openly. This was normal in the tribal areas. British troops were under strict orders to ensure that the only fire across the frontier was in direct response to guns firing on them. The post, in a house that was formerly the home of the local schoolmaster, was pockmarked by shot and shell.

Barbed wire entanglements stretched out into the desert heat haze on each side of the only open road between Aden and its desert hinterland, still a busy channel of trade with Yemen.

Camels were almost as numerous as cars at the near-by roadblock where every conveyance, every man, woman and child was searched for hidden arms.

The barbed wire was called the Scrubber line, after the nickname of an earlier sector commander who had designed it. It was a considerable hindrance to arms smugglers, though they frequently penetrated it. Ground patrols and interdictory fire from helicopters and rocket-firing Hunter jets made illegal crossings highly risky.

The road stretched back towards Aden through a litter of hovels and garbage, past a landmark known as 'grenade corner' in Sheik Othman, to a sandbagged, abandoned mission hospital called Fort Walsh. This was established as forward headquarters by the First Paras in a hard-fought battle that passed almost unnoticed amid the larger issues of the contemporary June War between Arab and Jew far to the north. One paratrooper was killed, and ten gunmen were known to have died, a reckoning made by a process known to Americans in Vietnam as a body count.

From this Beau Geste style fort, Lieutenant-Colonel Mike Walsh and his battalion maintained a British presence against repeated efforts of terrorists to turn Sheik Othman into a no-go area.

British patrols came under frequent fire from the Al Noor mosque in the main square, but repeated searches by Arab soldiers, supposedly liaising with the Paras, failed to produce either terrorists or arms. 'Only old men sleeping' they invariably reported.

A FLOSY ruse was to booby trap pictures of Nasser in the expectation that either British soldiers or their rival NLF enemies would tear them down. It failed with British soldiers. For all they cared the pictures might have been toothpaste advertisements.

There was little enough to laugh about in the soldiers' daily round of danger and discomfort but the bronzed youngsters from Britain rarely complained. Entertainment was almost totally lacking. Families with dateable daughters had all departed, bars were closed, even the rest area cinemas were re-running films shown time and again before. How neglected Tommy Atkins was – as ever – compared with his American counterpart! Bob Hope made an annual pilgrimage to entertain American troops in Vietnam. The British forces entertainment organization, ENSA, had difficulty sending concert touring parties to Aden because of fears for their safety. Agents of bigger show business names insisted on insurance premiums far beyond ENSA's budget. The *Daily Express* took up the idea of a campaign to send star entertainers to Aden. Stars like Tony Hancock, Hughie Green, Bob Monkhouse and Samantha Jones responded and brought a token of a nation's thanks as well as much-needed entertainment. None of them ever played to such audiences, never fed such a hunger for a blissfully forgetful night out.

A few weeks after this showbiz interlude Parliament in Westminster also showed some belated interest in the Britons fighting this nasty urban guerrilla war. An Armed Forces Act of 1966 was amended to define 'active service' as covering operations for the protection of lives and property 'elsewhere than in the United Kingdom'. Previously it had specified 'in a foreign country', which excluded the colonial territory of Aden and even the protected states of the hinterland. After suffering forty-nine dead and nearly six hundred wounded the young veterans of the Empire's last rearguard were officially 'on active service'.

This tardy recognition of the soldiers' task did not immediately end a disgraceful street procedure often carried out under the curious gaze of Arab crowds. British soldiers involved in searching Arab houses and shops were lined up in the street afterwards and ordered to turn out their pockets in the presence of Arab policemen. One soldier told me, 'We don't like it, but the officers say if we are not searched the shopkeepers will complain that we have pinched something.' An officer of the Prince of Wales Own Regiment explained, 'This is standard procedure. It is laid down in a Ministry of Defence pamphlet called "Keeping the Peace".' Other British units, including the Paras, the Royal Marine Commandos, the Argylls and the Lancashires took the view that this procedure was not applicable in the Aden situation.

A deputation of respected elderly citizens was despatched to Government House to complain that the tough attitude of British troops, particularly the Argylls, was spoiling what had been generally happy relations with the British. They were courteously received by Mr John Wilton, a senior official. At the same time leaflets were calling a general strike for next day to protest against British brutality.

A few nights earlier a motorized patrol of the Argylls gave hot pursuit to a white motor car from which indiscriminate fire had been directed at British family housing in Waterloo Lines. The car fled through the gates of the Queen Elizabeth Hospital, and the Argyll pursuers followed.

To do so they had crashed through metal gates of a compound where hospital staff and their families lived. When they left, with an Arab just admitted with gunshot wounds and two others found hiding in the grounds, all the non-British doctors and nurses walked out of the wards to protest against high-handed behaviour. The eighteen British staff were left alone to look after several hundred Arab patients in wards scarred by hundreds of terrorist wall slogans. The Arab staff of almost six hundred agreed to return to duty after an undertaking that an inquiry would be made by Mr Tom Oates, the Deputy High Commissioner . . . another report gathering dust somewhere in the archives, perhaps to be available under the thirty years rule in 1997.

The day after the strike Mr Wilton, indignant as a diplomat

can show himself to be, followed up his eve-of-strike discussions with the deputation, with a letter to Sheik Ali Muhamed Maktari, leader of the senior citizens.

Mr Wilton wrote, 'Any friend of Aden would be saddened by the situation he sees in Aden today. He would see hand grenades and other murderous weapons used daily in the streets to kill innocent and guilty men alike. Rival gangs fight one another regardless of the harm they do to British and Arab lives.

'We are not the cause of this state of affairs. This was shown clearly in Crater during the period when there were no British troops there. How many people were shot or kidnapped during those days? Probably no one knows. These small groups of reckless extremists are, as you know, engaged in a struggle for power; as independence approaches this struggle will not stop and I fear may become even more violent.

'May I draw your attention to the fact that yesterday, when there was a general strike in protest against the alleged brutality of the British troops, there were forty-one attacks made on members of the Security Forces with grenades, guns, rockets, etc., as a result of which three were injured (none, I am happy to say, seriously). In the whole day no single civilian casualty resulted from any actions of the British troops.

'Nor is it the British who have paralysed and destroyed the administrative, commercial and industrial life of Aden, which was formerly so prosperous. It is not the British who have burned and wrecked property worth thousands of pounds, placed bombs in the houses of innocent people, and reduced Aden's port – the source of most of its wealth – to such a condition that the shipping lines of the world are anxiously looking for an alternative.

'It is not the British who have driven up prices; it is not the British who last week caused a shipload of badly needed rice which had arrived in Aden to be sent away without being unloaded.

'Please do not think I raise these points in any spirit of bitterness or reproach. I say these things merely to point out that many of the evils from which Aden is suffering will not end with our departure.'

16 Sir Humphrey Foils a Coup

Early in July the Federal Government announced its appointment of a Prime Minister with the task of forming a broadly based provisional government until elections could be held in the wake of independence.

At that time Aden's Independence Day was provisionally fixed for 9 January 1968. The move for a broader government was made under pressure from Sir Humphrey Trevelyan who hoped that some of the more responsibly inclined terrorists might be persuaded to put down their guns and join a government in which the traditional rulers no longer monopolized power.

The Prime Minister designate was Hussein Ali Bayoumi, a handsome, well-groomed forty-five, whose business interests were wide and had included being editor-owner of a newspaper. He was already a somewhat controversial figure internationally as the Federal Information Minister who had refused to transmit the United Nations mission's TV message to the people of Aden a few months earlier. Bayoumi's efforts were a non-starter. The NLF denounced him in forthright terms as a British stooge, and die-hard despots of the Federal Government like the tough Sherif of Beihan purposefully opposed his endeavours. Mr Bayoumi, noted for his fine European tailoring, chose to wear a blue and white futah sarong at his first press conference. It was held at his extravagantly furnished home, a fortified villa in Khormaksar.

Ten tribal bodyguards lounged in the hall and passages of the house or in the garden, some alertly eyeing the guests, others playing cards. Bayoumi, chain-smoking beneath a whirring fan, said he had been discussing his cabinet throughout the previous night right up until lunchtime. He expected the Federal Government to step down within two weeks. He said that most of his cabinet would be Adenis, a sharp contrast to the present Federation cabinet which was dominated by up-country sheiks. He claimed a favourable response from local leaders of both FLOSY and NLF 'nationalist' groups. He added a confident prediction of an early end of what he enigmatically termed 'British terrorism', and independence sooner than the January deadline.

That same evening Radio Sanaa, mouthpiece of FLOSY, denounced any idea of a Bayoumi government as 'another British trick'. It urged Arabs to renew the struggle in 'the final battle for freedom'.

Two more weeks passed before Bayoumi admitted that his efforts to form a cabinet had failed. In a radio broadcast he complained that the prominent citizens of Aden whom he had hoped would serve in his cabinet had refused any role in his government. He added, 'they say their wives won't let them'. He went on to appeal for help in saving South Arabia from 'anarchy and political and economic ruin'.

Earlier NLF leaflets claimed the kidnapping of businessman Shafik Mahmoud Shamshan. According to the leaflets he had confessed to accepting the offer of a post in a Bayoumi cabinet and also revealed the names of seven others who had agreed to serve as ministers. The NLF warned that all would be executed.

One week later the Federal Government announced Bayoumi's dismissal. Bayoumi flew at once to see the Sherif of Beihan, the current alternating Chairman of the Federal Government's Supreme Council, and returned in a rage from the interview. He told the Press, 'The Federal Ministers have no right to relieve me of responsibility for forming a caretaker government. So far as I am concerned I am still Premier-designate.'

He drove straight from the airport to the radio and TV station where he used his authority as Federal Minister of Information to remove the announcement of his dismissal from the next news bulletin. It had gone out once on an earlier newscast made while he was flying back from Beihan.

Next day, after a stormy meeting between British officials and a delegation of the Federal Government, Bayoumi announced that he had accepted his dismissal as Premier-designate. He chose to stay on as Federal Minister of Information.

Bayoumi went on public record as warning that unless the British High Commissioner intervened, the Federal Government, of which he was a leading minister, would secure itself in power and bloodshed would continue.

That was precisely what the Federal Government set out to do. The traditional rulers made an immediate bid to take positive control of the situation, seeking to wrest power from the hands of the British authorities whose secret worldwide diplomatic manoeuvres they viewed with pardonable distrust.

The Federal Government chose a time when Sir Humphrey Trevelyan was absent at the United Nations in New York to blandly announce its intention to proclaim a new constitution of its own – tantamount to a Rhodesia-style UDI. The aim was to form a government chosen from delegates of the sixteen member states of the Federation, which would remain the legal government of South Arabia after independence. The constitution, promised within three weeks, was to provide for a president, a vice-president, with a prime minister and cabinet responsible to a single chamber of state representatives. Its only novelty was a clause barring state rulers themselves from holding Federal ministerial posts unless they previously abdicated their state prerogatives.

This represented a complete row-back from the rulers' earlier reluctant agreement to a more broadly based government of the kind being negotiated at that moment by Sir Humphrey Trevelyan, under United Nations auspices, in New York.

This bold move, virtually a coup against Government House and its absent 'viceroy', could only succeed on the basis of commanding the fire power of the Arab army. The rulers clearly misjudged the extent to which the officer corps of their army had been infiltrated by the nationalist organizations.

Sir Humphrey flew back to Aden and talked tough in the quiet steely way familiar to world political leaders like Chou En-lai, Gromyko and Khrushchev, Nasser and Iraq's megalomanic General Kassem. They were outclassed. The Federal rulers' plan to steam-roller their new constitution through by 15 August was dropped. It was to be heard of no more.

While its future was being decided by murder and mayhem in Aden, independence for the colony was the subject of interminable, futile debate at conferences behind closed doors around the world. Marathons of verbosity went on in New York, Cairo, Geneva, Beirut, Riyadh as well as in places more directly concerned . . . London, Federal Government offices in Al Ittihad, Government House in Aden, and in the lairs of terrorist leaders in Taiz, Sheik Othman and the NLF's newly established forward headquarters at Zingabar, thirty miles east along the shore accessible by vehicle from Aden only at low tide.

Aden suddenly felt itself to be the centre of world politics. This produced a chemistry of puffed up importance unhelpful to rational agreement among small-pool politicians. This communal megalomania had earlier complicated situations in Cyprus, Rhodesia and other petty states suddenly vaulted into the eye of international storms.

By September Sir Humphrey Trevelyan was ready to make a new effort to take firm control of the disintegrating situation. On 5 September he peremptorily sacked the Federal Government. He went on Aden Radio himself to announce that the Federal Government had 'ceased to function' and that Britain was ready to discuss the formation of a new caretaker government with the nationalists.

On the same day Lord Shackleton began a sort of Aden prototype of shuttle diplomacy that later became the hallmark of America's Henry Kissinger. He arrived in Beirut to call on the three-man United Nations mission on Aden, now safely ensconced in Suite 1027 of the luxury Phoenicia Hotel in a resort that was at that period a sort of Arabian Las Vegas.

He advised them of the new British initiative, and stressed its chief component, the total ouster of the Federal Government they themselves had adamantly refused to countenance on their disastrous visit to Aden five months earlier.

It had already been approved by Nasser, who now had common cause with the departing British in working for a successor government in Aden on broader lines in order to head off a monopoly control of power by the rogue NLF – now beginning to show its colours as ultra-Marxists, far to the left of Arab socialism. FLOSY, the party of Arab Socialist doctrines closely patterned on Nasser's ideas, was by now clearly losing the armed struggle. Its only hope of surviving at all in South Yemen was on a basis of power-sharing with the NLF.

FLOSY leaders took the first step towards this by announcing willingness to share government on a fifty-fifty basis with the NLF. This statement was FLOSY's first public recognition of the NLF's actual existence. Till this time they had persisted in their original stand that the NLF was an arm of British intelligence, a devilish device to divide the nationalist front.

The new Peace Plan was supposedly sponsored by President Nasser who at this time badly wanted to withdraw from Yemen. His hated puppet regime was disintegrating fast under growing support of republicans and weary royalists for a moderate regime fully independent of Cairo. The Peace Plan was fostered throughout the Arab world through the Cairo headquarters of the thirteen-nation Arab League. It was far from desirable, but from Britain's point of view it was the best bet for an orderly transfer of power

– and that was now the single objective of Britain's concluding role.

It became known as the Cairo Plan. There were four main points:

1. It called for a unified stand by both FLOSY and the NLF in rejection of the traditional rulers and lackey political parties;
2. Each of the nationalist organizations was to maintain autonomous status in domestic political activity;
3. The new line-up was to be called the United Front for the Liberation of Occupied South Yemen – UFLOSY.
4. Leadership was to be on equal basis between FLOSY and the NLF, and portfolios in the Independence Government were to be distributed between them on a fifty-fifty basis.

Cairo's *Al Ahram* newspaper, whose editor Mohamed Heikal was frequently a mouthpiece for President Nasser, commented, 'Unity of the two organizations with such similar principles and goals is the only way for fulfilment of genuine independence.'

Sheik Mohamed Farid, Foreign Minister in the dismissed Federal Government, was in Beirut when these events were revealed. He called at the St George's Hotel and succeeded in making a personal protest to Lord Shackleton at 'Britain's high handed political manoeuvres'. He told me as he came away from the meeting, 'I told Lord Shackleton that Britain had no statutory right to interfere in the South Arabian Government, and that I and my ministerial colleagues do not accept dismissal by Sir Humphrey Trevelyan, who has internal authority only in Aden, just one of sixteen member states of the Federation.'

Sheik Mohamed, dressed in well-tailored Savile Row, speaking the impeccable accent of the Oxford of the flannel bags era, added that he would urge his ministerial colleagues to gather in Riyadh to ask King Feisal of Saudi Arabia to take over Britain's protective role in South Arabia.

Most members of the deposed government were travelling abroad, ostensibly to get away from Aden, insufferably hot climatically as well as politically, for 'health reasons'. Even the untravelled, medieval Sherif of Beihan was already in Saudi Arabia, having fled across Royalist Yemen to take refuge there with a huge household and tribal following.

Sheik Mohamed went on defiantly, 'The only successor government we will give way to will be one in which all parties and elements in the country are represented. Recognition of an NLF government by Britain will mean civil war in South Arabia like the one in Yemen.'

17 Double Talk

The army is the key to power in every Arab country, and the leanings of the splendidly trained and equipped South Arabian Army were better assessed in Government House on an Aden clifftop than in the Federal Government seat at Al Ittihad a few miles out in the desert. This must have been the weightiest factor in Britain's hard-necked rejection of the Federal rulers so long after the people of Aden had themselves objected to having these scions of archaic tribal rule foisted on them.

On a brazenly realistic new policy of cut and run the British prepared to hand over to the men behind the murder and mayhem. Some of these were little more than political gangsters. A few, mostly in FLOSY's ranks, were more or less forced into armed opposition by Britain's past mistakes. There was, anyway, no future for well-meaning moderates in Arab politics. In Aden and its wild hinterland the first nationalist movement, the South Arabian League, influenced by men who owed their political aspirations to British education, had been swamped by the boost which premature announcement of Britain's total withdrawal gave to the revolutionary extremists and their backers in Cairo, Moscow and Peking.

The first move was to revoke the ban on the NLF as an illegal terrorist organization by recognizing it as a legitimate political movement. This brought an immediate response in the shape of an NLF leaflet declaring readiness to attend talks providing that Britain accepted United Nations resolutions on the future of Aden.

Oddly enough FLOSY, despite its terrorist campaign and rabble rousing, had never been officially proscribed. Hopes had lingered on in the environs of Government House, and particularly among Labour Government Ministers involved in Aden, that its leader, Abdullah al-Asnag, might yet return to the moderate fold and negotiate a reasonable agreement for independence.

At this stage little more was known about the NLF – originally OLOS, the Organization for the Liberation of the South – than that it was led by a collective believed to number fifteen faceless men. It was backed by some wealthy Aden merchants, a few younger sons of ruling tribal families, and suspected of having strong support in the army and the armed police. Like FLOSY it was originally encouraged, armed and trained by Egyptian military intelligence in the Yemen. Its members had become disillusioned by the Egyptian performance in Yemen, and turned towards the new Marxism emerging from the Cuban revolutionary experience. This they picked up from Palestinian terrorists of the Popular Front for the Liberation of Palestine which helped in training NLF commandos.

Feisal Al-Shaabi, an elderly Arab believed associated with the moribund South Arabian League, turned up in Cairo as a representative of the NLF ready to meet FLOSY leaders for exploratory talks on the basis of the Cairo Plan.

He was an uncle of the man who now emerged as military leader of the NLF, a bespectacled intellectual in his forties named Quahtan Al-Shaabi. He had a degree in agronomy from the Gordon College in the Sudan, and was employed as a colonial civil servant in agricultural aid programmes. In his spare time he had written a book called *British Imperialism in South Arabia*, published clandestinely through the auspices of the South Arabian League. He drifted away from SAL when it lost Egyptian support because of its lack of militancy, and turned to the Saudis instead. Ashaabi formed a literary club in Crater, and the NLF emerged from that. He began his guerrilla career under Egyptian command in the Radfan campaign of 1965.

By the end of September the NLF High Command announced through their usual nebulous channels – leaflets tossed around the streets – that they would send a delegation to talk with FLOSY in Cairo. The same leaflet urged an end of civil war, but contained the seeds of fruitless wrangling by declaring that the provisional government for independence should be formed by both parties 'according to their weight'.

The NLF clearly carried overwhelming weight. They had liberated fifteen of the twenty states of the old Aden Protectorate (only sixteen agreed to amalgamate in the federation, the others remained in their archaic state). The NLF also succeeded in splitting the FLOSY leadership by refusing to talk with a delegation that included its top leader, Abdullah al-Asnag.

While these political moves were afoot there had been a tacit lull on the military front. Three whole weeks passed without a single incident involving British troops.

The South Arabian Army had already taken over security duties in Little Aden. This passed without incident save for some minor squabbling over the occupation of desirable residences in the newly built Falaise cantonment. The Arab army had also taken over the township of Sheik Othman, enabling the First Paras to pull back into a line through even more inhospitable salt flats on the desert side of the airport perimeter. Their new role was to neutralize the area within mortar range of the airport's long runway. British troops held all other areas of the colony's territory. All needed to be retained in trustworthy hands, as their domination was necessary to any strategy of withdrawal under fire.

On the eve of the Cairo talks the NLF pointedly announced by pamphlet that it would settle for nothing less than 'immediate British withdrawal', indicating they would refuse to engage in any negotiations involving the British. Perhaps the NLF leaders were sensitive to FLOSY's sustained attempts to smear them as an offspring of British Intelligence. Clearly they meant to avoid any risk of later accusation that they treated with the British instead of carrying out their boast to drive them into the sea.

As the wrangling began in Cairo attacks on British troops were resumed. At the same time a new offensive was launched against remaining centres of FLOSY strength.

Contingency plans were dusted off in readiness for a failure of the Cairo talks, and an overnight total evacuation of all British nationals in a withdrawal under all-out Arab attack.

Sir Humphrey Trevelyan, in a statement aimed at the haggling negotiators in Cairo rather than to the listeners of Aden Radio, said, 'Independence is imminent, and there can be no advantage to South Arabia of a continued British presence. The British government sincerely hope that a representative body will be speedily formed to negotiate the final arrangements for independence, and are ready to enter into negotiations immediately.'

A senior official of Sir Humphrey's staff put it in blunter terms, 'There's no valid reason why British soldiers' lives should be hazarded further merely to buy time for these psychopathically quarrelsome people to develop a glimmer of reason.'

The remaining front-line battalions had already sent off packing cases containing mess silver and mementoes such as the Argylls' detailed model of the Crater district. A naval task force was assembling beyond the ocean horizon to cover the final pull-out. As Sir Humphrey's statement was released fresh soldiers from 42 Commando, based on Singapore, were landing by helicopter from the unseen naval task force to take up positions as the ultimate rearguard. With them, slung below giant helicopters for every Arab eye to see, came four 195 howitzers, heavier mobile artillery than Aden had seen before. They were dropped into the airport redoubt. The new troops took over positions in Steamer Point from the Prince of Wales Own Regiment of Yorkshire, flown out from Britain at a few hours' notice during the mutiny emergency three months before. On the left flank in Maalla, now a deserted canyon of vacant apartment blocks, were men of 45 Commando. Then came the Argylls in Crater and Khormaksar. On the furthest flank beyond the airport were the First Paras.

Driblets of news of continuing NLF triumph among the desert tribes added to the increasing nervousness of FLOSY's deeply worried adherents. Months earlier, when 45 Commando handed their walled camp at Dhala over to the Federal Army in the general British fall-back on Aden, the Emir of Dhala had expelled his British adviser, Mr Julian Paxton, and denounced the British as imperialists. Soon afterwards a tough hill fighter known as Ali Antar, respected by British troops and revered by tribesmen as a sort of Robin Hood, moved into the Emir's Palace. Federal soldiers in the near-by camp were reported to have remained 'magnificently aloof'.

As the Cairo talks began the NLF took over the fertile state of Kathiri, one of the states that refused to join the Federation, three hundred and fifty miles east of Aden. The Sultan and his family had already fled to exile in Saudi Arabia.

British officers serving in the Federal Army were going through a particularly nerve-testing time. Several were murdered, several had lucky escapes from attacks on them by their own soldiers. A major and the pilot of a helicopter detailed to take a ruler from Aden to his home state were both killed, and their bodies were buried with the burned-out helicopter in a hole excavated by bulldozer.

This happened as the NLF took control of South Arabia's second biggest city, Mukulla, 270 miles up the east coast from

Aden, capital of the Sultanate of Quaiti, one of four states of the old Aden Protectorate that had remained aloof to all blandishments to throw in its lot with the federation. Only a few months earlier Sir Humphrey Trevelyan had personally flown into Mukulla in an attempt to pressure the nineteen-year-old ruler into joining the federation so that Britain's perpetual treaty of protection could be taken over as a responsibility of the Federal Army. At that time Sultan Ghaleb Ben Awadh, ruler of a land bigger than Wales, recently back from schooling in England, was publicly conducting a Nasser-style auction offering his state as a base to the Soviet Union for a subsidy that at least matched the one and a quarter million pounds annual hand-out that Sir Humphrey threatened to end if he continued to go it alone outside the Federal embrace.

Two incidents in this first major centre to come under NLF control gave considerable worry to British Petroleum officials at Little Aden refinery. They were planning to continue operations after the British withdrawal with more than fifty British technical experts and managers staying in their jobs. This had already been cleared by the NLF in leaflets describing the oil men as 'good friends of the Arabs'. The Egyptians were also concerned since the refinery was mainly occupied with handling the output of Sinai oil production previously refined at the Suez facilities destroyed in the June War.

The first incident was the arrest of the captain of the British Petroleum chartered tanker, *Border Terrier,* after it had discharged its cargo at a BP depot in Mukulla.

The second was the hijacking of a French-owned charter plane from Djibouti at the airstrip of Riyan, close by Mukulla, which the RAF had recently left deserted. The pilot of the hijacked plane, Bernard Astraud, aged fifty-five, owner of Djibouti Airways, had just delivered £15,000 in wages from Government House for the Hadraumat Bedouin Legion, until lately a British-officered state army. He was ordered at gunpoint to fly trooping shuttles into the mountain town of Ashraf where, while their leaders talked of partnership in distant Cairo, the NLF were mounting an assault on one of the last remaining FLOSY strongholds outside Aden. M. Astraud strong-mindedly refused to fly his plane to Ashraf. He was beaten up and detained while his Pakistani co-pilot made three flights into Ashraf. Only after that was Captain Astraud allowed to take his plane back to Aden.

Just three months before, Captain Astraud had doubled the size of his bush pilot airline by buying four Dakotas of Aden Airways, when it closed down as a subsidiary of British Overseas Airways, for a knock-down price of £35,000.

Such was the anxiety of the British authorities for the safety of a third country national that the RAF sent Hunter jets, flying in pairs, to shadow the French-owned plane on the ground and in the air. Beverley aircraft flew eight-hour sorties in circles around the area relaying radio messages. This lavish tailing task was amply rewarded when a Beaver transporting evacuating equipment to a new headquarters at Bahrein was forced down at Riyan with engine trouble. The pilot of another Beaver, on a similar mission, landed after it in case it was necessary to evacuate the crew and abandon the aircraft and its load. Tribesmen swarmed around both planes firing rifles in the air in triumph. The technical fault was easily corrected but the tribesmen refused to allow either plane to move. Hunters turned from their high flying observation role to scatter the tribesmen by the most spectacular low level beat-up that these expert desert flyers had ever staged, and the planes succeeded in taking off without mishap.

These events, foreshadowing certain breakdown of the Cairo talks, were followed by developments in Aden that threatened an imminent bloodbath. FLOSY, apparently believing its own branding of the NLF as tools of British Intelligence, had made frequent appeals to Government House to use its 'good offices' on behalf of FLOSY men kidnapped by the NLF. Aswadi, the President of the Aden TUC, blamed the British for kidnapping fifteen of his members a few weeks earlier.

Now FLOSY made a last desperate bid to gain the backing of the people of Aden, having clearly lost out to the NLF everywhere outside the old colonial boundaries. The High Command of FLOSY gave a press conference to denounce the British for planning to impose an NLF government – men of the desert, beloved of British officials – on the people of Aden.

I was expecting a secret rendezvous with Abdullah Al-Asnag, the 'wanted' FLOSY leader, who was reputed to be in hiding in Aden since the NLF veto on his attending the talks in Cairo. My escort warned, 'Remember, no names, no photographs' as we climbed three flights of stairs in a white and green fronted villa behind an unkempt garden. Men in uniform stood all around the walls of a large room on the top of the villa. I began shaking hands with a number of men whose faces were known to me. My secret meeting was with eleven senior officers of the Aden Civil Police, and twenty-four officers of the South Arabian Army, including seven lieutenant-colonels. I recognized the only two men in civilian suits as senior CID officers.

A police superintendent put a cocked sten gun on the grey carpet in front of him as he sat with his back to the wall on my right. On the opposite wall an army captain held a big automatic pistol. Directly opposite sat the senior officers, nursing caps decked with badges of the British crown and the scrambled egg of high rank.

A lieutenant-colonel, sitting beside the Deputy Commissioner of Aden Civil Police, read a statement in Arabic, and I was handed a typed translation headed 'Press Release – FLOSY'. It charged Britain with 'fomenting civil war and bloodshed, with attempting to keep FLOSY out of power in favour of stooge elements of the NLF Britain conspires to leave behind in Aden'. It accused Britain of delivering 2000 German rifles to strengthen the NLF position in the interior town of Ataq where FLOSY had powerful support.

While this brazen admission of treachery by trusted paid officers of the crown was proceeding, Aden was suffering its worst day of violence since the Black Day of the June Massacre. Six Arabs and a young Briton on the staff of Sir Humphrey Trevelyan were shot dead. Grenades were tossed in every part of town.

Next day Sir Humphrey called in all the senior officers of the Aden police and the Federal army and gave them an angry lecture. Then he flew to London to persuade the government that Britain's only remaining role in Aden was to get out as fast as possible. British lives must no longer buy debating time for South Arabia's endlessly feuding politicians.

While Sir Humphrey, his title newly changed to Governor-General, was flying to London I cabled these comments from Aden:

'Every rooftop holds menace and it can be death to a Briton to park a car. Our troops are perilously stretched and thin on the ground. Open graves are already dug in gruesome anticipation of increasing demand.

'Doubtless it looks less pressing in the calm and quiet of Whitehall where the passing of each day is not counted with relief at still being alive . . . where perhaps too much expectation may yet linger around Nasser's new posture of friendliness and his promises to help damp down the bitter mischief his crushed ambitions wrought in this unhappy corner of Arabia.

'Britain has no responsibility for a state of anarchy manufactured in Cairo and now running wild. It is an Arab matter. They must be left to settle it among themselves – in their own way.'

18 Civil War

While a smokescreen of diplomatic optimism covered bitterly futile wrangling at the Cairo talks the tempo of killing in Aden mounted as NLF murder squads intensified efforts to eliminate FLOSY leaders and intimidate their supporters. Five colonels of the South Arabian Army sent President Nasser a cable asking him to use his 'good offices' to bring about an early agreement between the NLF and FLOSY in order to prevent civil war. They said the army would recognize the two organizations and nobody else as representatives of the people.

In Crater the Arab Armed Police of infamous memory reasserted themselves by establishing gun positions on the roofs of abandoned apartment buildings on Queen Arwa Road, overlooking the scene of the ambush four months earlier. Chief Superintendent Mohamed Ibrahim explained it was a move to prevent FLOSY forces crossing Main Pass to relieve the defeated remnant in Crater now holed up in a cul-de-sac, ironically fearful of the day the protection of the Argylls would be withdrawn. This was unacceptable to Colonel Mitchell. He advised the police somewhat cryptically that the only place he could guarantee the safety of any Arab policeman was within the police compound.

The British rearguard throughout Aden was put on general alert as the Argylls moved to take over the rooftop positions from the police. But the Armed Police withdrew back across the road to their barracks without incident. This development was welcome to the Argylls as they had left these key rooftops out of their network of observation posts in order not to unduly intimidate the police in the delicate relationship that was somehow sustained between them since the recapture of Crater. There was keen disappointment among many of the soldiers that the Armed Police chose not to fight, but the meek climb-down by the erstwhile

their posts and captured a terrorist house with a cache of arms. Three gunmen died and nine surrendered.

In a leaflet FLOSY accused the Arab army of siding with the NLF with the aim of setting up a military government that would co-operate with the British in a disguised continuation of imperialism. The first part of the allegation was undoubtedly true. In Sheik Othman earlier Arab soldiers had used mortars and heavy machine-guns to wipe out a FLOSY stronghold.

On the second day of the army's open intervention against FLOSY, soldiers of the Aulaqi tribe (which supported FLOSY) took off their uniforms and fought as civilians in defence of FLOSY headquarters in the Al Mansoura Hotel. The building was pulverized by ten seventy-six-millimetre shells from Saladin armoured cars. Apartment blocks around Sheik Othman market place were also flattened or left gaping open with sagging floors. Survivors fled across the desert to Little Aden.

British troops were put on amber alert, a state of readiness for immediate stand to, as this went on. There were fears for the safety of the British commander of the Arab army, Brigadier Jack Dye, as the army purged FLOSY elements among the officer corps. British Paras in neighbouring Champion Lines – close by the Arab army headquarters – were poised to go to his aid.

A former Aden finance minister was shot dead in an ambush on his way home by car from his executive job with British Petroleum at Little Aden after escaping twice earlier in the week, first from a bomb that destroyed one of his cars, then from the bombing of the Pagoda chinese restaurant which he had recently bought from its British founders. Another former minister was found dead in the street shot through the head.

Hundreds of FLOSY prisoners were herded into lorries and driven along the seashore to prison compounds at Zingabar.

After four days of bitter fighting the last pockets of FLOSY resistance were wiped out. The Arab army had done so with total ruthlessness, using its heavy arms without regard to causing civilian casualties among non-combatants and with no concern over property damage. Already its British training under the rules of 'minimum force' was eroded. The dead, including many women and children, will never be accurately known. The death toll certainly went high into three figures, and the wounded into many thousands.

On the fourth day FLOSY's last chance of outside help disappeared. The pro-Nasser regime of Marshal Sallal in near-by Yemen was finally ousted in an army coup.

That same night South Arabian army chiefs, suddenly rid of fears of Egyptian intervention to install a FLOSY government, declared themselves openly. They issued a statement calling on the NLF to open negotiations to take over 'total power' from Britain, and warned that the Arab Army of South Yemen, as they newly styled themselves, would oppose 'any other front or party which stood against the will of the people'. So ended 6 November, Aden's bloodiest day.

From dawn next day Aden's streets were filled with exuberant crowds and honking victory motorcades. British soldiers, whose natural reaction was to shoot on sight any Arab carrying a gun or grenade, were suddenly confronted with hundreds of Arabs brandishing Kalashnikovs, pistols and grenades as though they were sporting trophies. There was a tense ten minutes while the first such crowd was held back at gunpoint at the first roadblock in Maalla. Then came orders to withdraw into fortified positions and let the crowds pass. Aden was in fiesta after that with starred black-red-white-and-blue NLF flags everywhere . . . on cars, in shops, on lamp-posts. Vendors were even selling them to British troops in a sort of 'it's all over now' euphoria.

An exuberant second head waiter of the Crescent Hotel took me to meet the NLF military commander of Steamer Point, an ex-schoolteacher named Abdullah Farhan, twenty-nine years old and father of three. With him was a buxom young Arab woman introduced as Naga Mackawee, niece of the FLOSY leader and former Aden chief minister, herself an early staunch supporter of the NLF. Farhan, a slight figure with a thin pencil moustache, dressed in white shirt, grey trousers, pointed shoes, claimed total victory over FLOSY in his tiny rock-walled area of back streets behind the Crescent shopping parade. 'We killed six and arrested three hundred and fifty,' he boasted. He denied that British civilians gunned down in his sector, several of whom my guide had served in the hotel restaurant, were all victims of one lone gunman. But he promised, 'No more British civilians will be executed if the soldiers leave soon.'

Meanwhile the Arab army was mopping up a FLOSY pocket at the village of Bir Amed with .76 shells fired from its new Saracen armoured cars. All road blocks outside the British areas were manned by NLF youths while the army finished off their political

Grilling in the sun for captured
rioters in Armed Police barracks,
Crater.

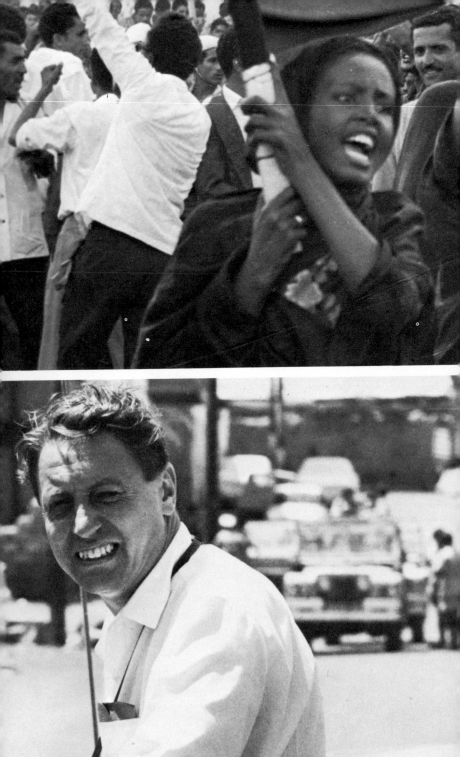

left Crater: Funeral of an Arab liberation hero.

below British reporter (the author) and bodyguard.

Street scenes in Aden's Crater district:
A banned procession disperses as the Northumberland Fusiliers
charge.

above A grenade explodes
below Then sniper fire.

left Rebel in uniform guards FLOSY, terrorist headquarters i Taiz, safe behind the Yemen frontier.

below A wounded Fusilier comforted by a comrade.

below *right* Angry member of same patrol makes arrest.

opposite:
above A British army boot restrains prisoner while his captor watches for rooftop snipe

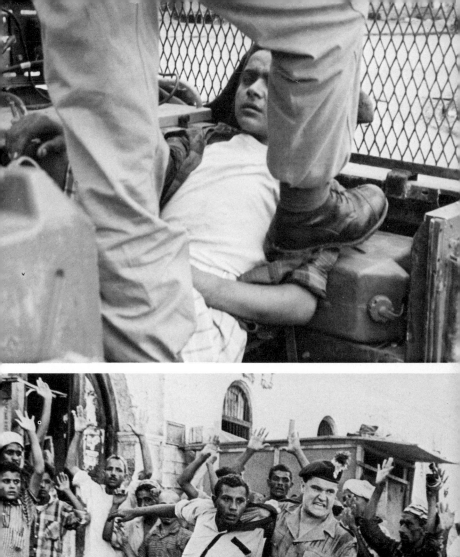

above Dubai before the oil era.

left Dubai after the oil strikes. Hunting falcons parked outside modern hotel.

rivals. Ten senior officers of the Aulaqi tribe, FLOSY sympathizers, were allowed to resign. The RAF flew them under safe conduct to the Aulaqi capital of Ataq.

From a new headquarters amid the ruins of Sheik Othman, Seif al Dhali called another press conference to announce that the next step must come from Britain. He said, 'Britain must make a public statement accepting the NLF as sole representative of the people before the NLF High Command will agree to talks that might lead to a ceasefire and orderly withdrawal.'

The awesome prospect of shouldering the responsibility of government was already modifying the language of bravado. There was more at stake than losing all hope of £50 million in aid that Britain had already promised to pay during the first three years of independence. This would provide transitional relief to an economy to which hitherto the British taxpayer had contributed £14 million of a £17 million annual budget. More important than this short-term pension was an uninterrupted flow of revenue from the British Petroleum refinery at Little Aden, now enjoying a boom by refining Egypt's oil production after the destruction of the Suez refineries. A total British evacuation that might include key British technicians, whose families had already left, would paralyse this lucrative operation. It was understood that they would only stay if a British Embassy remained to watch their interests. Suddenly the NLF were anxious that one Union Jack should remain flying in Aden – over a British Embassy.

That was the background to Seif al Dhali's threat, 'If Britain leaves us in the lurch, unless we are recognized as the sovereign government before Britain leaves, we shall never open relations, never entertain an embassy here.'

Sir Humphrey Trevelyan lost no time in recommending to the government in London that this should be acted on. Within three days direct talks between Britain and the NLF were being arranged to take place in Geneva, and 22 November was scheduled as the date for final British withdrawal.

Meanwhile, through its old routine channels, the Arab Army of South Yemen, still technically under the command of Brigadier Dye, asked for RAF strike support against incursions from Yemen. Incredibly such aid was forthcoming. In its last action in South Arabia the RAF attacked heavy mortar and machine-gun positions manned by the FLOSY Liberation Army near the border town of Kirsh, some sixty miles from Aden. Brigadier Dye was matter of fact about it. He explained, 'At the request of operational commanders I passed on a request for RAF support and it was cleared immediately. The first strike was made at 8.30 a.m. Only two strikes were needed. The planes hit entrenched mortar and heavy machine-gun positions.' The Hunters, destined for sale to the Jordanian air force to replace similar aircraft destroyed in the June War, had been delayed in Aden after scheduled departure in case they might have been needed to repel attacks on British forces by heavy units of the army which sought this final air support.

At its headquarters in Seederseer Lines the Arab army was still purging political waverers. Seventy officers and NCOs – much of the cream of years of British training – were sacked. Some of them joined FLOSY supporters in the prison pens along the coast at Zingabar.

Brigadier Dye told me over a drink in his villa in Lake Lines, 'The situation is more tense than it's ever been, more dangerous than last June.'

19 The Assassin of Steamer Point

While the familiar fabric of the old leisurely colonial life disintegrated around them British civilians, businessmen and government officials, carried on as normally as they were able. Wisely they rarely ventured from the Steamer Point area which was largely free of the gun battles and riots familiar in other districts of Aden until a month before the end. Months before that, however, there was nowhere in Aden where a lone European walked in greater peril than in the streets and alleys around the duty-free shops, the shipping offices and banks of the Crescent. Here a lone killer with a 6.75 Chinese automatic pistol killed fourteen Europeans in the last months of British rule. The technique was always the same; a target of opportunity and two shots at close range in the back of the head. There was some speculation that these cowardly killings may have been caused by a paranoid assassin taking advantage of the break down in law and order. However, the NLF proudly claimed each victim's death as an execution.

The word assassin, itself, comes from these feuding badlands

advance from the shipping agency of Luke Thomas around the corner.

'Now the crumpled body has a name – Johanne Theison, master of the tiny Danish tanker *Stainless Carrier* (219 tons), a frequent caller at Aden Port.

'He is carried away to the morgue and I retrace his last steps through fifty yards of shopping arcade on the safe side of a wire and wall barricade that shuts off the Arab back streets from the modern offices of Luke Thomas, shipping agents.

'There on a desk in a third floor office that overlooks his ship in the harbour lie three letters waiting to be posted to Denmark, and an 8mm colour cinefilm to be sent for processing and returned to an address in Copenhagen.

'But the news of his death reaches his family faster than any telegram. His wife and two toddler daughters live aboard the little ship in the harbour.'

The NLF claimed his killing as the execution of a British agent.

Only two of the known victims of the Steamer Point assassin survived his shots. One was bank accountant Mr Michael Booth, shot as he sat in the front passenger seat of a car about to drive away from the British Bank of the Middle East. The bullet hit him in the neck and passed out of his cheek. The driver, bank manager Brian Thomas, threw himself into the road and drew his pistol. When he got up there was nobody about except two Arab police-men standing fifty yards away and making no move to help. Earlier an Arab official of the bank had been shot dead, and an Indian assistant manager left Aden after twenty years when he received a death threat.

The second target of the Steamer Point assassin was widower Alan MacDonald, a familiar figure reading a paperback thriller in the Crescent Hotel where he had lived for years. I was in the dining-room when I heard three shots fired at him as he was leaving the near-by annex on his way to dinner carrying a thriller called *Time of Fear*. Two bullets passed cleanly through him, but he managed to grapple with the gunman on the annex steps. He made a full recovery. But the thwarted killer struck again next morning against the Danish ship's captain whose death is described above.

Each night by this time the Crescent area with its gardens and soccer pitch was made a no-man's land. Gun battles raged furiously with thousands of rounds of ammunition whining and pinging around every building as NLF gunmen poured concentrated fire into every British position on a front of four hundred yards. Mortars landed around the hotel. Flares hovered against rock faces above the alleys behind the Crescent arcade. Tracer patterned the sky and bullets seared the dust of the soccer pitch in front of the hotel, a sort of midfield grandstand between NLF rooftop positions and Canute barracks, headquarters of 42 Commando and an attachment of the King's Own Borderers. The British gunners were virtually pinned down with the harbour at their backs.

British positions behind the Crescent had been abandoned after an incident in mid-October in which wounded British soldiers had to wait ninety minutes for medical aid. Their observation post was barely three hundred yards from the main road through Steamer Point, but it took a force of three hundred infantry with three armoured cars to evacuate them.

This attack came while talks were still continuing in Cairo. It was part of an NLF offensive to commemorate the fourth anniversary of the date they name as the beginning of Aden's liberation, 15 October 1963. The date's significance is a mystery. Nothing particular passed on that date.

All hopes among the British of salvaging some kind of working relationship into the uncertain future seemed to be ebbing fast. The calculated gamble for staying on was getting to look like madness. There seemed no prospect of saner days ahead.

When the last BOAC flight left Khormaksar airport on 31 October it was given full-scale air, land and sea protection. The First Paras covered the Arab army's positions in Champion Lines, the only pocket of potential danger inside the defence perimeter. Hunter fighters, armed with rockets, gave top cover, poised to strafe any gun or mortar position that opened fire. Four helicopters, heavy machine-guns panning, patrolled the airport perimeters. Two miles offshore the Commando Carrier, HMS *Albion*, was in direct line with the runway in case the airliner was damaged and forced to ditch.

Among the passengers were ten nurses from the Queen Elizabeth Hospital, Aden's only hospital for civilians. They were leaving reluctantly under firm orders because, badly needed as their services were, the risks of continuing their work were judged unacceptable. British battle casualties were already being treated in a one-hundred-bed hospital aboard HMS *Albion* where two

RAF nursing sisters, Flying Officers Sheila Glen and Sue Quinn, were making history as the first women on active service afloat with the Royal Navy. The last women members of the armed forces ashore had been evacuated a month before from jobs in Middle East headquarters.

Two Yorkshire surplus dealers were among departing members of the British community. They were sadder and wiser men having paid £100,000 for 1100 surplus vehicles and barrack furniture which the NLF refused to let them ship away.

Earlier when Aden Airways closed down as a BOAC subsidiary, costing £70,000 a year in subsidies, a Viscount airliner was burned after its last scheduled flight because it was being sent back to London for disposal.

As withdrawal date approached bounties, paid by the British on weapons and ammunition handed in, were drastically scaled down. The price for mortars and rockets dropped from £600 to £100, machine-guns from £400 to £100, pistols from £50 to £10, hand grenades from £25 to £10, landmines from £120 to £50. A British official explained, 'We don't want a last-minute rush to turn plentiful arms into badly needed cash.'

A few British women still remained after this last civil flight from Aden. Some were secretaries like Barbara Stone, of St Helens, Lancs., who drove to her job in the Federal Ministry of Health every day with a .38 Smith and Wesson revolver on the seat beside her. She and others were apparently overlooked, and were evacuated in a military plane a few days later. That left a few oil wives who stubbornly refused to leave their husbands in Little Aden, and several British women married to Arabs. These families were offered facilities to settle in Britain.

As the Steamer Point area became increasingly swept by cross-fire, military headquarters, scaled down for a much reduced role, moved to Bahrein. Senior commanders of the rearguard worked from makeshift offices inside the airport perimeter. Remaining civilians, including a growing group of international newsmen and foreign consular officials, were allocated lodgings in empty army villas on Tarshyne beach within the maximum security perimeter. The Red Cross representative remained alone in the Crescent Hotel.

Contingency plans were ready for the evacuation of all Britons and one hundred and thirty-four foreign nationals. The list included thirty pilots and groundstaff engaged by the commercial company Airwork to operate the new state's emerging air force.

Meanwhile in the long tradition of Imperial ingratitude – shades of Aden's founder, Commander Haines – British officials on short-term contract received formal notice of dismissal under terms which cheated them of paid leave. One of them commented, 'We think this is just about as stingy as even a British government can get – especially when the dependants of a detained terrorist get £30 a month from the British taxpayer.'

It was even then looking as though Britain's one continuing building project in Aden, a structure solid as a pillbox gun position intended to house a British Embassy, would be yet another waste of money. Pictures of the Queen were taken down and crated ready to be carried away in an evacuation from near-by Tarshyne beach.

Then came more stirring news. The magic words 'The Navy's here' flashed around the tiny British community as the powerful silhouette of the strike carrier, HMS *Eagle,* and an armada of twenty-five other ships appeared on the horizon late on the after-noon of 6 November. Suddenly the vast emptiness of the Indian Ocean had become a close and safe haven.

This was followed by British recognition of the NLF as the successor government, and an announcement that direct negotia-tions were to begin immediately in Geneva.

On the same day the NLF issued the first revolutionary decrees. These were clearly aimed at reassuring the technicians whose departure under a general British withdrawal would have killed what remained of Aden's economy. The decrees branded looters as criminals, and guaranteed the safety of foreign communities and the security of private and business property and commercial assets.

20 Operation of War

The NLF's correct behaviour in Little Aden, where operations at the oil refinery were running smoothly, helped greatly to restore a feeling of more confidence among the few Britishers and foreigners contemplating remaining in business in Aden after independence. Those permanent inhabitants whose entire exist-ence had to be bound up in Aden were caught up in the joyous euphoria of NLF supporters. NLF flags sprouted on every bicycle, car, from every window. Whatever the future might hold there was enormous relief that the daily horrors of murder and street fighting seemed to lie behind them. Years of peace and prosperity that had ended only with the beginning of terrorism three years before were all but forgotten like the ghosts of memories long past, almost legendary. It had become a fixed idea in most Arab minds that it was the presence of British soldiers that caused such horrors, and so to them the answer was quite simple: remove the British soldiers and the horrors would disappear too. A few Britons, Government officials and businessmen, especially oilmen in their artificial, encapsulated company town of Little Aden, spoke such thoughts openly.

It's a bit like saying that policemen create criminals. Yet without police there can be no law, no hope of justice, no community order. Perhaps that is to over-simplify. But so is the argument that a British military presence is counter-productive to safeguarding British interests because it serves as a catalyst for agitation. In the Aden situation it was the ill-considered decision to announce a deadline for withdrawal that fanned the flames of violent rivalry for political power into a murderous civil war. British troops were whipping boys for both sides in the real struggle fought out so ruthlessly among the Arabs themselves.

All was set for the last British soldier to leave Aden to its new NLF masters on 22 November when an urgent request came for the troops to stay longer. It came from the NLF! This astounding development came on the morning of 13 November in time – thanks to a clock difference of three hours – to prevent Mr George Brown announcing it in Parliament. This early date was aimed at preventing talks with the NLF at Geneva becoming bogged down in marathon haggling over detail. British delegates were instructed to get the NLF delegation to agree to a simple joint document recognizing the NLF leaders as rulers of a sovereign South Yemen Republic.

This independence document, probably the simplest of its kind ever visualized, was also to have contained a simple statement providing for a British Mission to stay on in Aden to continue negotiations with the new independent government about future relations and outstanding technical matters like aid, new currency backing, gratuities to civil servants. Britain nursed hopes of limiting the Geneva talks to two days – surely aimed at making the

Guinness Book of Records – and was expecting that its decision to end forthwith its responsibilities for Aden, already merely nominal, would add considerable boost to rapid general agreement. The one remaining British interest was to avoid a bloodbath withdrawal and keep a tenuous diplomatic toehold through the boisterous transition period in hopes of improved relations in more settled days. The old native rulers, who believed themselves betrayed by Britain's unilateral revocation of perpetual treaties of protection, had by now either fled or joined the NLF bandwagon.

Sir Humphrey Trevelyan's contacts with the NLF were through the Arab army's Chief of Staff, Colonel Ahmed Mohamed Hasani, and the Deputy Commissioner of Police, Colonel Abdullah Saleh, whose NLF *nom de guerre* 'Sabah' was well known to British Intelligence. They were asked to call at Government House on the morning of 13 November to be advised, as a courtesy, the withdrawal date which the Foreign Secretary would be announcing in Parliament later that day.

Within ten minutes they were speeding back the three miles to the headquarters of the Arab army, now the hub of all NLF operations, political and military. Soon their pleas for the withdrawal to be delayed were cabled to London. The two colonels told Sir Humphrey it was impossible to get the NLF delegation to Geneva for talks to begin on 15 November. They explained that some members of the NLF delegation were in Beirut, others in Algiers, and not easily or swiftly contactable.

The real reason, of course, went much deeper. It had to do with cash . . . as much cash as the NLF could squeeze out of Britain for what they termed 'compensation for one hundred and twenty-nine years of colonial exploitation and oppression'. It had suddenly dawned on them that Britain's wish for a peaceful withdrawal was the only real asset left in their hands. If there were no British troops as 'hostages' to NLF attack left in Aden then there would be no safe conduct left to barter over. The oil refinery, now back on full production with crude shipments from Egypt, was economically vital to an independence economy, only now a useful adjunct of overseas commerce to Britain – and so a bartering asset to Britain rather than to the NLF. A mere handful of last-ditch British businessmen would hardly be hostage enough for the many millions the NLF were demanding as compensation.

The NLF leaders had learned in exile that in matters of aid the countries of the Eastern Bloc, suppliers of encouragement and plentiful weaponry during the armed struggle against Britain, were far less forthcoming and more demanding of collateral than the imperialist countries of the West.

So the British rearguard, poised and ready to withdraw any time, was ordered to extend its stay for eight more dangerous days . . . a hundred and ninety-two more perilous hours. The postponement, supposedly till 30 November, was bitterly resented by troops of the rearguard, now slimmed down to six thousand men with an air transport operation, bigger than anything since the Berlin airlift, ready to begin. The troops resented being used as pawns in political point-making. Only two days earlier a marine commando was severely wounded when the NLF turned from triumphant motorcading to break the tacit truce with a heavy mortar and machine-gun attack on British positions. This was intended to hustle formal recognition of NLF rule by Britain which London was then being laggardly about. It was also a fierce demonstration of the hazards of a fighting withdrawal under the kind of heavy barrage of firepower the NLF militia, unaided by the Arab army, could put up.

An official at Government House commented on this reversion to gun barrel diplomacy by the NLF somewhat wryly. He said, 'They are shooting away what little prospect remains of them getting the £50 million in defence and development aid we pledged to a successor government.' Of this sum, vast in days when the pound was still buoyant, £32 million was earmarked for military aid spread over three years to finance a military self-defence capability that would provide an alternative to the old treaties making Britain responsible for protection from external attack.

While mortars and bullets crumped and buzzed around British soldiers, British officials at the civil airport terminal were already carrying out an NLF decree that nobody must leave the country without an exit permit. An Indian with a passport as 'citizen of the UK and colonies' was turned back from a plane to Bombay. This order was later amended to refuse exit to passengers unable to prove payment of income tax. Access to the departure areas of the airport, like the perimeter, was still rigorously guarded by British troops and passengers were searched by British security personnel. A British spokesman declared with almost forgotten firmness of language, 'No interference with a British subject will be tolerated.'

While Lord Shackleton and his aides in the British delegation kicked their heels waiting for the NLF delegates to gather in Geneva, Britain opened the gates of its centre for political detainees at Al Mansour. Out into the sunlight came thirty-one well-groomed, well-fed Arabs – all hard-core terrorists held on positive evidence of murder. Ten of them were carried shoulder high in an NLF victory parade headed by a shining new Toyota van owned by the contractor who had prospered on twelve shillings a day allowance for each prisoner's meals. During their detention prisoners' families had been receiving weekly allowances varying from £3.50 to £17.50 according to a scale based on normal income. Soon after smiling handshakes with their British jailers they began relating stories of British brutality totally at variance with their sleek appearance. Mohamed Qabati, forty-three-year-old former clerk with a British shipping agency, emerged from two years' detention. He gloated, 'We are happy to come out and find we have beaten the English.'

The other twenty-one were glumly unsmiling. They were losers, members of FLOSY, likely to be torn apart by NLF mobs outside the prison gates. They were lifted over the streets of their homeland in two RAF helicopters to the airport where a special Egyptian airliner waited to fly them straight into exile in Cairo.

Dressed either in neatly pressed suits or freshly laundered futah sarongs and shirts, they clutched cigarette packs, and staunchly refused to say anything other than thanks to Red Cross representatives who arranged their immediate evacuation. British soldiers guarding the helicopter pad thought they were the NLF delegation to the Geneva talks!

Meanwhile Sir Humphrey Trevelyan was moving out of his palatial quarters in Government House so that it could be made ready for its next inhabitant. 'We must leave it in perfect order,' he said. 'No, I feel no pangs at leaving. It's time we all went.'

He was packing three personal suitcases to see him through the last days before he left for London via an RAF lift to Bahrein. Packed with his spare clothing were books by Dostoevsky, in Russian, and Kafka. The peacocks that graced the grounds had already gone to the more plebeian environs of Sheik Othman Zoo. Cannon first mounted under the supervision of the first resident, Commander Haines, had been shipped to the National Maritime Museum at Greenwich. Everything carrying the royal cipher, which meant most of the crockery and cutlery, had also been shipped to Britain. Everything else, including priceless carpets covering the sprung floor of a huge ballroom, was left in place.

Gone, too, were the pennants and tangled radio antennae above the vast hilltop bungalow from which Middle East Command had controlled British forces throughout the Indian Ocean and the Persian Gulf; including operations to rescue the newly independent presidents of Kenya, Tanzania and Uganda from their own mutinous armies; the Kuwaiti rescue; the Rhodesian sanctions blockade. With them had gone folders of contingency plans for similar operations that may have arisen in the area in the future, including evacuations of British nationals from such situations as Uganda. Without Aden all these plans are now academic.

Gone also were thousands of unit plaques from barrack walls. Gone were the polo ponies, perhaps as much a symbol of past glories as a globally respected Union Jack.

A statue of Queen Victoria that had frowned on Crescent Gardens through more than half the period of British rule in Aden was removed at dead of night in a parody of Sir John Moore's funeral at La Corunna. It had been saved from a secret burial at sea originally planned for it, and it was remounted on an obscure site where its stone features could glower back at rock cliffs surrounding a nearly completed building expected to house a post independence British Embassy.

The embryo embassy was, in fact, a tiny custom-made fortress, and men detailed to stay behind with a handful of diplomats as security watchmen were highly trained in weaponry. The safety of its staff was to be further supported by a special naval force ordered to remain out of sight offshore for months if necessary, ready to land on near-by Tarshyne beach for a fighting evacuation. In the event the embassy stayed on without any critical incident, though it was later invited to find new premises in Khormaksar.

The official value of buildings left vacant was rated at £26 million, far below cost. There were also twenty-six soccer pitches, thirteen cricket pitches, and two huge air-conditioned bowling alleys completed in 1964 at a cost of £70,000.

A blind official eye was turned while British troops arranged to leave memorials of their passing Aden's way that would not easily be erased. The RAF lifted two huge red, white and blue harbour buoys to the 1700 foot summit of Mount Shamshan, and chained them deep in concrete. Men of 45 Commando left a huge White Ensign on an unclimbable crag overlooking Maalla. A private car was left perched on top of another peak.

Sir Humphrey lodged briefly in Aden's most famed building folly, a round house close to Government House, built at a cost of £40,000 a few years earlier to house the Admiral. His last night – which happened to be his sixty-second birthday – was spent aboard the strike carrier, HMS *Eagle,* riding at anchor offshore.

There was one last great parade of British power before the end – discreetly beyond the reach of any exuberant gunmen who might have been tempted to join in. The Governor-General reviewed the evacuation fleet, an occasion unmatched in size since the Coronation Spithead Review of 1953. Eight warships, nine Royal Fleet Auxiliaries, seven Landing Ships (Logistics) and one Landing Ship (Tanks) lay at anchor in the outer harbour in four lines astern of Elephant Back Light. It took an hour for Sir Humphrey, aboard the minesweeper HMS *Appleton,* to take the salute of each ship, receiving three cheers from crews lining the decks in tropical white. The crashing roar of a seventeen-gun salute echoed around the rock faces of Aden.

Then Sir Humphrey boarded the flagship, HMS *Intrepid,* for a fly past of Buccaneer strike bombers, Sea Vixens, Gannets and helicopters. It was something more than a ceremonial display. The roaring jet planes and the gun salute backed up a warning from the shore operations commander, Brigadier Richard Jeffries, to the NLF commanders of the Arab army.

He had advised them that British forces would 'hit back hard with all we have at any serious attempt to interfere with our withdrawal'. It was also made clear that in such an eventuality the Arab headquarters and barracks would be primary targets. The military, at any rate, had got the measure of the Arab mentality.

The first part of a three-phased final withdrawal, planned as 'an operation of war', was completed by dawn on 26 November, a full twenty-four hours ahead of schedule.

This was my description of the withdrawal from Crater written at the time:

'Silent figures emerge from the deep shadows of King Solomon Street, pause to whisper their names to a figure with a list and a shaded torch, then pass in file through sandbagged positions and into three-ton lorries waiting at the end of Marine Drive. One tall figure in a glengarry stage whispers "at last" as he climbs over a tailboard on his way home to Scotland.

'Beyond open windows above the wary heads of soldiers padding Crater's streets for the last time ceiling fans spin idling in the light of a bright half moon. Suddenly a little dog barks. A soldier clasps its jaw in a firm grip and quietly pats and calms the tail-wagging camp follower.

'As cowed Crater sleeps the Argyll and Sutherland Highlanders withdraw as they came in just one hundred and forty-six days ago – by surprise and without a casualty.

'Major Ian Mackay, aged thirty-three, D company commander, packs up his headquarters in flats formerly occupied by British bank clerks. He makes a final check of two-tier bunks left smart as for daily inspection. We share a last glass of orange juice from left-over stock of four bottles. He picks up a half-read paperback entitled *Caen* left open print down on a table, and we leave.

'The major switches off the fans but leaves the lights burning as they normally are throughout the night. Maps and orders are left on the walls. The major clicks the door quietly behind him, pistol in hand ready for use.

'We walk softly through shadowy streets. Two soldiers covering us from behind sight a moving shadow that turns out to be a goat. Memories flicker of mobs and grenades and sniper fire – days of tension and terror.

'Twenty-five men of D company hold the "Highland Line", a perimeter established for the last hour of British rule in Crater. Major Mackay speaks softly with each man, whispering final orders. Armoured cars of the Queen's Own Hussars wait in shadows near-by to take them out when everybody else is clear.

'Private John McCulloch, aged twenty-six, of Stirling, lies full length behind the cover of a low wall. Not long to go now before the odds that he will live to see the three-months-old daughter born since he came here rise enormously. But these last minutes of danger hang heavier than ever before.

'Suddenly the deep silence ends, the skirl of Scottish pipes startles the sleeping crows from a near-by shrubbery. Pipe Major KennethRobson, another Stirling man, plays "The Barren Rocks of Aden" as the Argylls' regimental flag is lowered from the commanding position on top of the Chartered Bank. The inimitable Colonel Colin Mitchell leaves his headquarters in proud style.

'For John McCulloch, behind that low wall, the music means

just fifteen more minutes on active service in Crater. Cruel past months mingle with thoughts of joyful reunion ahead. Three of his regiment, including his original company commander, died in the Arab police ambush soon after they arrived in Aden last June. Two more died in mortar, grenade and gun attacks during one hundred and twenty incidents. Twenty-four others were wounded. But he was safely waiting to board a plane home before unbelieving Arabs came sleepily into the streets to find that Crater was no longer under the stern rule of the Scots.'

At the same time as the Argylls slipped out of Crater 42 Commando and C company of the King's Own Borderers were abandoning their positions in the Crescent area of Steamer Point and the high-rise apartments of Maalla, covered by more armoured cars of the Queen's Own Hussars. An astonished Arab army colonel in Maalla was handed a huge bunch of keys and told that the rents for 1700 apartments had been paid till the end of the year although most had been empty since June.

This left only one company of commandos guarding the new embassy building outside the wide perimeter around Khormaksar airport.

By this time the airlift of troops to Bahrein and onward transit to London was fully under way lifting out a thousand a day. The garrison was stripped down to three thousand five hundred front-line soldiers.

Brigadier Jack Dye, the thirteenth and last commander of the British-trained Arab soldiers of the hinterland, toured the positions taken over by his soldiers after the British had withdrawn. Then he returned to Khormaksar to hand over his command to Colonel Mohamed Ahmed Aulaqi, a respected professional soldier who had spent nine years in the ranks before being commissioned seventeen years earlier. He wore the MC won in a Yemen frontier skirmish ten years before.

It was a small formal ceremony held on the perimeter between the British airport defences and the Arab army headquarters cantonment. It was the only part of Aden not bristling with guns. The Arab honour guard was unarmed, so were British senior officers and their escorts. The only visible weapons were Kalashnikov machine-guns carried by the bodyguard of the Aden Police Commissioner, Abdul Hadi, now brazenly revealing himself as a prominent NLF leader in a predominantly FLOSY police force. Brigadier Dye took the salute of a march past of eight camels, an old world touch, and then with a loud sigh of relief left the ceremony to board a plane.

Meanwhile the streets were filling with exuberant crowds and the NLF announced it was taking 'provisional measures of government on the basis of information that the British were leaving on 28 November'. They announced the name of the new state as The People's Republic of South Yemen. Among its first measures was the introduction of visas for foreigners 'to replace the illegal documents of imperialism'.

Throughout the day planes of the airlift shuttled through the runway as naval aircraft patrolled high above and helicopters prowled the perimeter wire. By afternoon the last planeload of Argylls was gone.

Just before sunset figures came out of the saltpans from the direction of Sheik Othman and swarmed at the far end of the runway like an apparition in the heat haze. They had cut the perimeter wire and come through trailing rifles. More than five hundred dusted off their red berets, formed ranks of eight abreast and marched straight down the runway. A patrolling helicopter dipped in salute. A middle-aged RAF man, dressed only in tropical shorts, stood on the tarmac watching, tears of pride streaming down his face.

The First Paras, young veterans of eight hundred terrorist assaults with rockets, mortars, grenades and machine-guns in the Sheik Othman hellhole, came out of the harsh saltpan positions they called the Pennine Chain. They were smart and proud as on passing out parade. A thin line of green-bereted men of 42 Commando had relieved them in the discomfort of their Pennine Chain line. The battalion commander, Lieutenant-Colonel Mike Walsh, marched at their head. He explained, 'We wanted to show that three months of tedious duty holding a quiet line since we pulled back from Sheik Othman has not made us in the least slipshod.'

General Sir Philip Tower, himself a para, took the salute. He told them, 'You have lived up to the standards set by your predecessors at Arnhem. You have stuck out months and months in horrible conditions.' The First Paras had captured one hundred and twenty-eight terrorists, lost three killed and twenty-five wounded. They were flown homewards in a continuous stream of RAF transport planes that landed and took off through all that night.

On the morning of 28 November compo rations for twenty-four hours were handed to soldiers of 42 Commando and the King's

Own Borderers as the last cookhouse wallahs and Naafi canteen managers emplaned for home.

Sir Humphrey Trevelyan arrived by helicopter from his night with the fleet, held a small farewell reception in the departure lounge of the RAF's own little terminal, and inspected a guard of honour drawn from all three services. A Royal Marine band in ceremonial pith helmets gave the occasion a piquant colonial touch as they played the aptly chosen tunes, 'Puppet on a String' and 'Fings Ain't What They Used to Be'.

As an RAF Britannia flew the 'last viceroy' to Bahrein the British Forces Broadcasting Station, which relayed the BBC, went off the air with the National Anthem . . . all three verses including the pointed words, 'confound their politics, frustrate their knavish tricks'.

21 'Tearful, Ain't It'

Soon after Sir Humphrey Trevelyan's plane headed off safely towards Bahrein a head-shattering clang of metal rang out across the airport. RAF technicians armed with huge sledge hammers pounded secret transmitters into twisted hunks of shapeless metal in the only wilful destruction by the British of the mountains of equipment it abandoned.

Throughout the day planes came and went ferrying seven hundred men of 45 Commando to Bahrein. Already Khormaksar – till recently the busiest RAF airport in the world – was a ghost town of deserted barrack huts and bungalows with swinging doors and shutters. Arab house boys, flush with severance payments, laden with household goods given to them by the departing Sahibs, crowded at an NLF roadblock across the airport road, emerging beyond it with lighter loads and pockets.

Aden's streets were almost deserted when I drove to Khormaksar from the Crescent Hotel that last morning. The night had been quiet save for the drone of planes as the airlift went on. The last three huge transports took off one after the other at lunchtime – 10.40 GMT. They carried the last of the portable communications equipment, weary-eyed RAF traffic control personnel and other RAF groundstaff, and the military top brass.

One bronzed youngster expressed a typical soldier's farewell as he walked up the gangway. He said, 'Fucking tearful, ain't it!'

They lumbered down the long runway, and were soon safely out over the sea climbing towards Bahrein. Behind them were two empty Argosy transports that had flown from Bahrein and not landed. They had been sent as spare capacity in case of a mechanical breakdown among the last three aircraft.

As they disappeared a fluttering, throbbing cloud of helicopters moved in from the sea, splitting out of formation towards individual objectives. Commandos climbed drop ladders to board them from lonely piquet posts on Aden's peaks, others moved back from sandbagged positions on the airport perimeter wire. Within half an hour a reduced perimeter was held by a hundred and ten men of the King's Own Borderers, the gallant Charlie Company whose honour this was. Men of 42 Commando pulled back on the last British redoubt, the clubhouse of the Aden golf and polo club, now massively sandbagged and nicknamed 'Fort Alamo'. The flagpole had been cut down from the exposed roof, and re-erected where men lowering the flag for the last time would have better protection and a quick sprint to their helicopter.

At 11.20 GMT the yellow and green flag of 42 Commando was pulled down, signifying that the last guardians of the perimeter were safely lifted out. Fort Alamo was abandoned under the cover of guns from the desert golf course's twelfth 'brown', the last holding position.

A line of army lorries was heading towards it, but stopped several hundred yards short of Fort Alamo. The warning that the Royal Navy's strike planes and big guns were at action alert had successfully deterred Arab plans to give the last British troops a gunshot farewell.

As the rearguard commander, Lieutenant-Commander Dai Morgan, of 42 Commando, backed into the last Wasp helicopter the NLF flag broke over Fort Alamo.

The last view these soldiers had from their weaving helicopters was an apt summing-up of the entire British experience in Aden from its founding as a bustling port by Commander Haines till this bitter end.

Beneath the NLF flag Arab junior officers were gesticulating around the military vehicles parked, ignition keys in place, by their recent British owners around Fort Alamo. They were quarrelling over their new ownership.

22 Welcome British Soldier

Almost two years before Britain's evacuation of Aden the young Ruler of Bahrein, Sheik Isa al Khalifa, had suggested during a press interview with me that Britain should move the Middle East base to his own island realm half-way up the Persian Gulf.

'The British are more than welcome to move their base here,' he said. 'We know who our friends are. We do not have four faces. Our relationship with Britain is the corner-stone of our life. The British stand for law and order, for steady development. We have seen too many countries turn the British away, and then lapse into chaos.'

His next words undermined these splendid sentiments, many might say invalidated them, from a comfortable western philosophic point of view. Replying to my questions he made it clear that he rejected any idea of broadening the basis of the government and the judicial system to end the exclusive monopoly of both by his own relatives – a state of affairs for which Britain had long been bitterly blamed by merchants, students and oil workers whose disparate interests were linked in a common resentment of exclusion from a voice in public affairs which lifelong contacts with Britain had taught them to expect.

Since the mid-twenties Bahrein had enjoyed the most socially progressive regime in all Arabia. This was due to a remarkable Englishman, officially unconnected with the British Government, who became adviser to Sheik Isa's father after answering an advertisement in the Personal Column of *The Times*. He managed Bahrein like a bailiff might manage a squire's estate in England while his wife pioneered education, hospitals and other good works.

He had been able to achieve on the limited oil revenues of Bahrein what the more limited resources available to the Colonial Government of Aden had barely toyed with. But this great and good man was also an autocrat. The paternalist style of sheikly rule suited the task of his lifetime, but he failed to see that political advancement was a necessary corollary of social and economic progress. This failure, this development of one without the other, encouraged revolutionary change. Trouble had begun ten years before, during the full flood of Nasserism, and had been damped down at the eleventh hour only by the intervention of British troops. The scapegoat for the riots was the Sheik's adviser, the alien *éminence grise* behind the throne, Sir Charles Belgrave.

His name, sadly, is not revered in Bahrein as it should be. His memorial is invisible, as such. It is the predominance of the role Bahrein and educated Bahreinis play in commerce and administration throughout the Gulf. For instance, the United Arab Emirates' first ambassador in London was a Bahreini (and still is at this time of writing), though Bahrein stood disdainfully apart from fabulously rich mainland desert neighbours when the new United Arab Emirates was formed from seven previously insignificant sheikdoms.

At this 1965 interview Sheik Isa – the name is the Arabic form of Jesus – clung to the views of his father which Sir Charles had neglected to modify. In less developed countries they might well be the only realistic view, even today. 'An assembly,' he smiled, 'would be merely a platform for agitators who would ask the British to quit. People who talk of such things are like sheep . . . show them grass and they will go to it even if it is to be slaughtered.' He added, innocent of irony in the words, 'Anyway, we have a chamber of commerce.'

There was a selection of eight brands of filter cigarettes on the coffee table in the glittering audience chamber of the desert palace where his stable of fine horses was far removed from the pervading grime of the oil refinery. We drank first coffee, then black tea from tiny handleless cups. Bowing servants poured liquidized frankincense from elegant brass jugs over our hands and held a pot of scented embers for drying. Sheik Isa, a small, dumpy figure, wore full desert robes with triple gold headband. I left him at the end of an hour anxious to telephone his son at school in Cambridge.

When I had interviewed the previous ruler a decade earlier mobs had been rampaging through the streets of Manama, the capital, demanding that the British Adviser go home. During this visit I found that even diehard pan-Arabists were worried that the British devil they knew might suddenly leave them to the rival mercies of medieval Saudi Arabia – 'people of the desert' as Bahreinis contemptuously called their brother Arabs on the mainland – and the Shah of Persia, both claimants to sovereignty over it.

Two years after this interview with Sheik Isa, during the last stages of the Aden withdrawal, Mr Goronwy Roberts, Minister of State at the Foreign Office, flew to Bahrein to reassure Sheik Isa that there was no question of British withdrawal from the

Gulf. He had gone on to reassure tribal leaders in Qatar and the seven Trucial States of the lower Gulf that Britain would not renege on protective treaties with them as it had with the protected states of the Aden hinterland. Booming prosperity everywhere had smothered all trace of pan-Arab nationalism even among the imported workers from Palestinian refugee camps. Under a crash building programme a new British army base was shaping at Sharjah, close by a long-established RAF staging post airfield. The British military presence in the Gulf, based on Bahrein and Sharjah, was being doubled to a total complement of six thousand men. Not, of course, that another exhibition of the British genius for barrack building was any more an indication of real British intentions than it had been in Aden and many other British military bases of historic recollection. British promises were not what they were when an Englishman's word was universally respected as his bond . . . forgetting in this wide context some glaring embarrassments like the promises to Arabs and Jews over Palestine.

Two months after his first tour Mr Goronwy Roberts, since ennobled, visited the Gulf again to advise the rulers that his earlier assurances had been somewhat premature. The question of withdrawal from the Gulf had now, indeed, come up, and the Gulf rulers should know that Britain would be completing a total military withdrawal from the area within four years.

Despite years of rumour and nightmare fears this sharp reversal of policy stunned the rulers of all the states with which Britain had treaty relations. Most worried of all was Sheik Isa of Bahrein. The future looked fraught with peril. The Shah, with a vast modern military machine at his command, claimed the island sheikdom as the fourteenth province of Iran, making its ruler a rebellious vassal who had traitorously helped maintain illegal occupation by British forces.

Bahrein is separated from the Saudi Arabian coast by fourteen miles of coral shallows, and from Iran by one hundred and eighty miles of deep sea. All that remains of the Persian paramountcy that followed expulsion of the Portuguese in the seventeenth century is a proliferation of Persian family names and a strain in the blood most notable in the Bahreinis' haughty attitude of superiority to their nomadic desert neighbours. Warrior ancestors of the ruling al Khalifa family from the near-by Qatar peninsula drove the Persians out in 1783.

Even so the Shah's tenuous claim was seriously maintained to the point of refusing the validity of foreign passports that carried any trace of passage through Bahrein immigration control. Iranian maps still include the island sheikdom within the Shah's new empire.

Against this background Sheik Isa acted with uncharacteristic urgency when he became convinced that the British really did mean to carry through the unthinkable, and leave little Bahrein to its fate. He decided to seek alternative protection from the lesser local devil, and flew off to Riyadh for emergency talks with King Feisal of Saudi Arabia.

King Feisal, already worried by revolutionary Arab neighbours on his southern and north-eastern land frontiers, acted to dissuade his fellow 'reactionary', the Shah, from any impetuous attempt to establish his military might on the southern shores of the Persian Gulf, known throughout the Arab world as the Arab Gulf. Barely twenty-four hours after the public announcement of Britain's intention to withdraw from all military commitments East of Suez, King Feisal pledged his fullest support, in all fields, to Bahrein. This came, fortuitously, only a few weeks before a long-scheduled state visit to Saudi Arabia by the Shah. During that visit the two autocrats decided their mutual interests as major oil producers, upholders of traditional status quo in an area simmering with perilous change, were more important than a quarrel over the Bahrein bone.

Eventually the Shah agreed to waive his claims to Bahrein in exchange for British recognition of his sovereignty over three small uninhabited islands in the middle of the Gulf which Britain had looked after in the interests of Sharjah and Ras al Khaima, tiny pocket states under British protection which could lay claim to some nominal sovereignty over them.

While Sheik Isa was away in Riyadh I talked with his cousin, Sheik Mohamed bin Mubarek al Khalifa, in his capacity as Information Minister. He told me sorrowfully, 'Only a few weeks ago we were assured by a British government minister that British forces would be here indefinitely for our protection. It is quite shocking. It leaves us without an umbrella. It's like expelling Italy from NATO, but worse because we are a tiny country and have never felt the need to have an army of our own.' Sheik Mohamed, four years younger than the thirty-seven-year-old ruler, educated at London University, said Britain and the United States ought to help maintain stability in the Gulf because of their own vast oil interests. 'Scratch a match here,' he added, 'and you set fire to the whole area.'

Bahrein first entered into Treaty relationship with Britain in 1820 when the ruling sheik requested the island's inclusion in a General Treaty of Peace which the East India Company's warships imposed on the states of the old Pirate Coast, changing the geographical name to the Trucial Coast. In 1861, when Bahrein was threatened with invasion from the near-by Arab mainland, Britain guaranteed Bahrein's independence, and the ruler under-took to abstain from piracy and slave trading.

Towards the end of the nineteenth century Britain's imperial rivals, particularly the latecoming Germany of the Kaiser, mounted serious intrigues throughout the Middle East. The British, ever mindful of the defence of India, reacted by securing her century of domination of the ancient east-west trade route through the Persian Gulf. In 1892 a new series of 'Exclusive Treaties' were signed with the Ruler of Bahrein and with the seven Trucial States. This brought them fully under British protection from renewed pressures from the Ottoman Turks, the Persians and a dynamic Muslim revival under the Wahabis of the desert interior of Arabia. The rulers each pledged, 'I will on no account enter into any agreement or correspondence with any power other than the British government.' This effectively kept out diplomats and agents of rival powers, sealing the area as a tribal reservation with British wardens.

So it remained into the present – a closed area where even innocent travellers were closely vetted and journalists could be banned by the political resident based in Bahrein, employed by the Foreign Office. This gave officials an enviable freedom from any restraints of public surveillance, and thus from the hazards of Parliamentary debate. Apart from handfuls of air travellers overnighting in Sharjah or Bahrein, itinerant traders peddling luxury items to sheikly families, few Britons and hardly any nationals of other lands had any idea of this backwater of Britain's imperial role.

This situation remained long after the first oil strike in the Gulf was made at Bahrein in 1932. That signified the beginning of the end of an idyllic life for young Britons enraptured by the Arab way of life, and for the people of an area mostly poised on the edge of harsh poverty. With the influx of oil workers, labourers from Persia, displaced persons from Palestine, as well as foremen and managers from Britain and America, came marvels of creature comforts like air conditioning and refrigeration to transform life in an almost insufferably hot and humid climate. Other seeds of immense change were sown by free education in schools built with wisely spent oil revenues, and scholarships to higher education in Britain and America. For want of better harvesting, the thrust of this new element in the Bahrein community came near to boiling over disastrously during the heady heyday of President Nasser's pan-Arab nationalism. The dreams of a great new Arab empire, the bitter racism of constant incitement against Israel, leapt the barriers of distance and local censorship to the transistor radios which Bahrein merchants were importing along with other delights of mass production and the consumer age.

The first stirring of revolt came in the mid-fifties from the trade unions formed in the oil refinery at Awali. It was led by a former Arab executive of a British bank.

Ostensibly the agitation was aimed at the alien behind the throne, Sir Charles Belgrave, the sheik's adviser and commandant of police. The Ruler himself was too fearful a figure to criticize directly, and enjoyed worshipful loyalty from the general population. The political leaders, frustrated by the obscurantist nature of the closed society, determined to attract attention in Britain to their claims for a voice in public affairs. The opportunity came when Mr Selwyn Lloyd, then Foreign Secretary, called in at Bahrein where his plane needed to refuel on his way to India and Pakistan. His car, and the cars of his party, were heavily stoned during riots specially staged for his visit. All that emerged immediately to the outside world was a paragraph in *The Times* playing down the incident and describing the rioters as an exuberant football crowd. It happened that the Bahrein correspondent of *The Times* was Sir Charles Belgrave. The only other newspaper correspondent in Bahrein, which had no local paper at the time, was James Hamed Belgrave, son of the Ruler's adviser. He was 'stringer' for the United Press news agency but neglected to file a word about the most sensational event in Bahrein for decades. He was also the Bahrein government's official censor as I was to find out soon after I flew in from New Delhi where the Foreign Secretary's visibly bruised and battered party told me of their tribulations and the fury of the mob.

Bahrein was in tumult for weeks. British troops were called into the streets on internal security duties, and a Royal Navy cruiser raced to Bahrein at top speed in a demonstration of gunboat diplomacy. Sir Charles ceased forthwith to represent the London *Times*, but it was two years before the old ruler reluctantly gave way to pressures – from London as well as from the mob – for his retirement as sheik's adviser. A sad close to an admirable life's work.

Trade unions, banned from that time, are still technically forbidden, though they openly exist. An attempt in 1975 to drape the family autocracy with the trappings of representative democracy by means of a partially representative National Council, was short lived. In that 1968 interview Sheik Mohamed had forecast, 'Your system would bring anarchy. We are in the Middle East, not Europe. Our kind of system works here.'

The search for oil had focused on the Middle East after the Russians struck it rich at Baku in the Caucasus in 1873. By World War One this ugly, evil-smelling liquid was already an essential element of the opening motor-car civilization. More important at the time it was vital to the operations of the new iron-clad navies, key to sea power.

The development of major oil fields in Persia and new strikes in Iraq quickened interest in the Gulf area. Under the treaties the Gulf Rulers were unable to negotiate concessions without British agreement. This power was not used to make Gulf oil a British monopoly. The Bahrein concession was originally acquired by a British syndicate in 1925 but was taken over by Standard Oil of America in 1931. They struck oil a year later and a refinery built near the oil field was exporting ten thousand barrels a day by 1936. Revenues, modest against oil incomes of later-developed fields, were used from the beginning to benefit the population at large and put Bahrein with a clear lead as the most civilized centre in the Gulf; a lead still maintained.

Inevitably Britain was drawn into the internal affairs of the Gulf states way beyond the intention of the original treaties. The new communities of foreigners, many non-Muslims, brought social and economic problems beyond the understanding of tribal courts and outside the competence of local administrations. A special judiciary, presided over by British officials, was set up for foreigners because the tribal courts meted out justice according to the Koranic Shari'a – the holy way of life.

It was 1899 before Britain extended its protection policy to take in a mud-walled town at the northern extreme of the Gulf when it came under threat of attack from the rising power of the Saudi emirs. Thus the prosperous pearl-trading harbour of Kuwait and 7500 square miles of desert sand at the top of the Gulf came under British paramountcy. This move was inspired by the *Drang Nacht Osten* (Drive to the East) policy initiated by the German Kaiser. He was pushing a project for a Berlin-to-Baghdad railway, and his agents were stirring resentment of British influence throughout Persia and Iraq to the very borders of India.

In the opening years of the Nasser era Kuwait had changed little in a half century of British influence. The old mud walls were yet to fall victim to massed legions of bulldozers beginning to fill the desert air with raucous noise, raising a permanent dust cloud over a mutilated terrain far from the desert oil field causing it all. In 1956 there was no hotel. I stayed at a sort of pension at the top of narrow stone stairs from the old covered souk. It was called the International Trading Agency. The rooms were primitive but the food, supervised by a Swiss manager, was a delight. My bare little cell overlooked the courtyard of a newly built mosque surmounted by a neon-lit crescent.

The showpiece of modernization was a short stretch of neon-lit dual carriageway along which members of the ruling Sabah family drove their new Cadillacs. The fabulous revenues were just beginning to show. Royalties were then a mere £200,000 a day, but the sheikly regime was already a target for Nasser's ambition. The sheik's security police dealt harshly with attempts to form demonstrations, and foreign oil workers, who included many Palestinians, were deported at any suggestion of political trouble-stirring. Egyptians were employed in every branch of a mushrooming administration. They were the doctors and dentists manning shiny new chrome equipment in half-finished hospitals. They were training police, training a newly formed army, training Kuwaiti students as pilots, teaching in newly opened schools. The policy of hiring the opposition was beginning.

Buying off enemies is a hallowed tradition in an area where bribery at every level of government is still an expected practice whether the transaction is for a new driving licence or the purchase of a multi-million-pound defence contract. Loyalty under such a system tends to last only until a higher bidder comes along. So it was natural that the Kuwaiti ruling family, with a steely realistic view of human nature notable even in a Middle East context, should begin looking for a main chance as signs gathered of

Britain's declining power in the area.

From the time of Britain's shameful climbdown at Suez in 1956 Kuwait followed a policy of distancing itself from what had become a politically embarrassing relationship with a country widely denounced as the arch-enemy of the Arabs. This policy accelerated after the overthrow of the pro-western regime in neighbouring Iraq. They had already discovered that Nasser had a price for toning down his scathing propaganda. They reckoned that every other Arab revolutionary had his price too. Kuwaiti policy was based on tough repression of internal dissent, paternal coddling of the tiny population, strict working permit control of foreigners, and buying friends in most unlikely circles in the outside world. With the exception of one near-fatal error this cynical belief in the total power of wealth has been successfully followed to date.

Kuwaiti was cleared of any stigma of serving as British stooges when the Exclusive Treaty of 1899 was formally abrogated by an exchange of letters dated 19 June 1961. But, in keeping with Kuwait's practice of backing every horse in every race, these letters of exchange replaced the old treaty with a secret defensive alliance, cleverly wrapped up in the sub-clauses. Only the ending of the old treaty was mentioned in the rigidly controlled media.

The Kuwaitis had miscalculated the kind of man who ruled next door Iraq. Within days of the treaty's abrogation the crazed Iraqi dictator, General Kassem, moved troops across the desert towards Kuwait and asserted Iraq's claim to the golden patch of desert just beyond frontiers drawn by British imperialists after World War One.

In panic the Kuwaiti ruler called for British help, and British paratroopers were rapidly airlifted to Kuwait and dug into a defensive desert line across the Iraqis' line of march. Oh! the embarrassment of it, the arch-enemy of all the Arabs having to save one tiny defenceless Arab state from a bigger brother Arab state! The Arab world was loud in protest, and after the danger was past the British expeditionary force was withdrawn and replaced by a token force representing the Arab League of which the potential aggressor was one of thirteen members. Two years and many handsome handouts later Kuwait was admitted to full membership of the United Nations and its independence was formally recognized by Iraq after the murderous overthrow of Kassem. We shall see in a following chapter how the grotesquely wealthy little sheikdom of Kuwait showed its gratitude to the country that twice saved it from conquest, not to mention Britain's role in developing its unearned multi-billions.

On 13 May 1968 Kuwait Radio announced that by mutual agreement the 1961 defensive treaty with Britain was terminated. In fact notice of termination was handed to the British Government on that date, and the treaty remained an ultimate reassurance to Kuwait for three more years, expiring finally on 13 May 1971.

Almost three score years and ten before that all the Arab nobility of the Gulf area and far inland gathered in Kuwait to meet Lord Curzon, Viceroy of India, at a great durbar. The ambitious Kaiser was then posing a menacing threat to British interests, and the Arab east was ruled then and for a long time into the present century by British officials under the control of the Government of India in New Delhi.

Curzon told his colourful audience of desert princes, emirs and sheiks, 'We were here before any power in modern times showed his face in these waters. We found strife and created order. It was our commerce as well as your security that was threatened. We saved you from extinction at the hands of your neighbours. We opened the seas to the ships of all nations. We have not seized or held your territories; we have not destroyed your independence, but preserved it. We are not going to throw a century of enterprise away.'

Half a century later, in April 1957, such an ardent anti-colonialist as C. L. Sulzberger, owner and roving reporter of the *New York Times*, wrote that the only alternative to dangerous anti-Western Arab imperialism (he meant Nasserism, but at that time it was State Department policy to soft talk the Egyptian leader, then at the height of his pan-Arab popularity) was the continuation of the Victorian British protective system in the Gulf. This meant propping up the personal rule of sheiks while influencing them towards better treatment of their peoples than was to be found in non-protected Arab states. He concluded, 'It is a paradox of this anti-colonial era that if Britain's Empire were suddenly to relinquish its appanages in the Persian Gulf, NATO and the Free World might collapse.'

23 Soldiers for Hire

Eastward from Bahrein on a desert peninsula the sheikdom of Qatar was bustling with exploding riches from newly discovered oil wells far, far richer than the comparative trickle that had made Bahrein the envy of its smaller neighbours for so long. The population leapt from 20,000 Bedouin herdsmen to 60,000 almost overnight. It had come under British protection only after the retreat of the Turkish garrisons in 1916, and the country remained into the sixties as poor and backward as Bahrein was bursting with modern ideas along with its hospitals and schools, cars and refrigerators.

Further east beyond Qatar stretched a sparsely populated chain of tribal territories, lining the old Pirate Coast, known as the Trucial States since the Royal Navy cleaned out the pirate bases and established Britain's General Treaty of Peace in 1820. Most developed of these was the State of Dubai whose ruler, Sheik Rashid, was a shrewd merchant prince with an astute Bahreini, Mahdi Al-Tajir, an old boy of Preston Grammar School, as his chief of customs and excise. Long before oil was struck there in the late 1960s Dubai port was prospering – mainly from a huge transit trade in gold bullion smuggled into India and Pakistan where financial controls enormously inflated its inherent value.

Doubling back westwards from Dubai we find Abu Dhabi with a Bedouin population of about 30,000 dotted across a wide area of inland desert. In the late sixties it was undergoing the topsy-turvy traumas of fabulous oil strikes and an income almost beyond imagination. Well within the decade its per capita income was to be highest in the world at almost £12,000 a year.

Clustered in a quilt of pockets of territory at the base of the Muscat peninsula at the Indian Ocean end of the Gulf were the lesser sheikdoms of Ajman, resourcefully gathering in windfalls of foreign exchange from frequent special issues of postage stamps for the adornment of tens of thousands of schoolboy stamp albums around the world; Sharjah, where the port was silted up through disuse, and a main source of income for twenty-five years had been rents and salaries provided by a small RAF staging air-field dating from the pioneer flights of Imperial Airways; and the even poorer sheikdoms of Umm al Qaiwain; Ras al Khaimah; and Fujairah.

The British presence had brought peace but little change in terms of social development. Its motive had been strategic defence of the Indian Empire and nothing else. The Gulf was the shortest east-west trade route since ancient times. It was the maritime outlet of Persia and Iraq. It was obviously necessary to exclude other European powers from such a beckoning gateway to India.

This rainless littoral on the Gulf's southerly and easterly shores was cut off from effective domination by more powerful tribal groupings in the interior of the Arabian Peninsula by vast stretches of desert, the notorious wilderness known as the Empty Quarter. Till the British came, lawlessness, piracy and slave trading prevailed among the petty rulers and freebooting adventurers and outlaws from many lands. This was the legendary coast of Sinbad the Sailor and Aladdin's Cave.

Britain emerged from earlier commercial rivalries with the omnipresent Portuguese and Dutch to become the predominant power in the area throughout the nineteenth century. British warships destroyed a powerful pirate fleet which preyed on shipping passing through the Straits of Hormuz between the Gulf and the Indian Ocean, and followed through to raze a pirate fortress at Ras al Khaimah. These operations were immediately followed by submission by the rulers of the coast to the Trucial Treaty of 1820. The Sheik of Bahrein, who then also ruled his ancestral homeland of Qatar on the neighbouring mainland, signed the treaty voluntarily. Under it all the rulers undertook co-operation with Britain in suppressing piracy and the slave trade. Specifically excluded from Britain's return obligations was any involvement with aggression from the Arab interior.

From this time Britain won the plaudits of the enlightened world for its role in reducing the flow of African slaves into Arabia from a level of open and profitable trading on a huge scale to an undercover business of smuggling that exists as a trickle even to this day.

Growing pressures from the Ottoman Turks, Persians and the fanatically puritan Muslim Wahabis who were later to found Saudi Arabia, led to increased British involvement. In 1892 the Trucial States and Bahrein signed 'Exclusive Treaties' with Britain by which the rulers each pledged, 'I will on no account enter into any agreement or correspondence with any power other than the British Government.' But within the ring of this protection Abu Dhabi and Dubai were virtually at war with each other as recently as the late forties, though the battles were little more than occasional clashes. It took three years of patient mediation by political agents to sort out this quarrel between neighbours. There were no moves to establish schools or hospitals, and no possibilities that the impecunious ruling families could provide the kind of developments Sir Charles Belgrave was pursuing in Bahrein from the latter twenties. European governments had no overseas development programmes in those days, and the Gulf was a little-known appendage of the Indian Empire.

The attitude of the officials chosen to shoulder Britain's responsibilities was an important factor in leaving the area in its primeval natural state. They liked it that way. They learned the native Arabic dialects, the tribal customs and enjoyed playing a viceregal role in feudal societies.

The coming of oil spoiled it all. It brought a huge influx of foreigners to win the oil from below the desert sands and the offshore coral reefs, and another wave after that to build the palaces, dual carriageways, schools, hospitals, barracks and all the other monuments of material prosperity. Inevitably it brought need of greater internal security forces, and social and economic problems among the foreign communities for whom Britain was responsible in international law. British courts were set up in a special legal system governing foreigners. Late in the day, with more than enough funds available, Britain was able to influence the introduction of more efficient methods of government and progressive social policies.

Inevitably this interference in internal affairs brought the British authorities into dispute with rulers unable to adjust to this whirlwind of change.

One of these was Sheik Shakhbut ibn Sultan, whose leisurely life of ruling thirty thousand Bedouin, hunting with falcon and composing poetry, was shattered by the discovery of oil. From the beginning he was suspicious of the high prices the oilmen offered, and it took these sharp business men many months to persuade him to accept double the value he put on his cut from the companies. Then he insisted on payment in coin and folding money. He progressed to accepting revenues in gold bullion only when rats ate huge quantities of his stored currency. But he steadfastly refused to allow the vast fortune to change his country's way of life, and was eventually transported to exile in London aboard one of

Her Majesty's frigates of the Royal Navy. By that time the gold bullion he had acquired in preference to printed credits in a bank statement brought Abu Dhabi a gain of more than two million sterling even at the low level of royalties he had been persuaded to accept, when the British pound was devalued shortly after his ousting!

The new ruler, Sheik Zayad, a younger brother, opened the floodgates to construction gangs in a crash development programme that has since transformed the desert, and swamped the original Arab population in a wave of immigrants from many other lands. It was already happening when Britain's decision to abrogate the old treaties added a new dimension to financing and development. Defence against envious neighbours and internal subversion became primary items for expenditure of the oil revenues.

Sheik Zayad was immensely admired by the British for turning down a bribe of £30 million from Saudi Arabia when he was governor of Buraimi Oasis. ARAMCO, the immensely rich Saudi-American oil partnership, smelt oil in the sprawling oasis of Buraimi deep among the ocean of sands in Abu Dhabi's interior, partly over the unmarked border with neighbouring Oman. In August 1952, a Saudi official with a military escort took up residence in one of the Oman villages of the Oasis, and began buying allegiance to Saudi Arabia although the nearest habitable areas of Saudi Arabia were some two hundred miles west on the other side of the Empty Quarter. Britain contested the Saudi claim to Buraimi, on behalf of its joint owners, Abu Dhabi and the Sultan of Muscat and Oman, in the International Court. This ended in a diplomatic row when Britain accused the Saudis of trying to fix the verdict of international judges.

Meanwhile Britain had formed an Arab *gendarmerie* called the Trucial Oman Scouts to police all seven of the Trucial States. It was financed through the War Office in London and directed by the Political Agent in the territory. The officers, NCOs and technicians were British, seconded from the British Army.

In October 1955, together with British-officered units of the Oman Sultan's army, the Trucial Scouts moved to evict the Saudi forces long entrenched among the lush pools and palm groves of Buraimi. Something approaching two hundred thousand rounds were fired in a day-long battle and one Arab was killed before the Saudis fled in their Aramco trucks. King Saud reacted by breaking off diplomatic relations with Britain – a break that lasted into the mid-sixties and the coming of a more enlightened government under King Feisal.

When I visited Buraimi by RAF Twin Pioneer supply plane in 1965 the Trucial Oman Scouts patrolled the rolling sand ridges of the petrified ocean on the edge of the Empty Quarter from a picturesque white-washed mud fort. The chief of the local Dawhir tribe, a fierce blackbeard named Sheik Sultan Ben Suroor, told me, 'The peace that the Inglesi has brought is good. Now our guns are for hunting. I pray to Allah that my children's children will still have the Inglesi here as their brothers.' He had refused a bribe of £4000, a massive sum before the oil strike had enabled him to add a bright red Cadillac to his stable.

I was surprised to find an American presence well rooted among the sweet water wells and irrigated palm plantations, unmarred by oil exploration rigs.

A missionary group from Chicago had built a hospital there, and staffed it with ten dedicated women nurses and two male doctors. Sheik Shakhbut, shrewd as ever, attracted the badly needed hospital there by allowing the missionary medicals to evangelize. In five years they had made one convert – an Arab employed in the dispensary – but the busy maternity ward was bringing more than fifty new Muslims into the world each month!

Buraimi's first bank had just opened in a mud-walled little house. Mr Tony Whittam, a bachelor from Exeter, was finding it an interesting job. 'They will perch their falcons on the edge of my in-tray while they write their cheques,' he said.

My travels around Buraimi took me into the domain of the Sultan of Muscat and Oman, ruler of a land then tightly closed to foreigners, visited by less than a handful of journalists who had agreed to maintain silence on some aspects of events there.

Britain's relationship with Sultan Said bin Taimur was vague, almost as secret as the recurring guerrilla wars and tribal revolts endemic to the area. Regular British Army officers were seconded to the Sultan's Army, directly under the Sultan's command. British policy was to keep the Sultan sweet, presumably because Muscat dominates the southern shores of the Straits of Hormuz and Britain maintained RAF staging airfields at Salilah on the coast of the embattled Dhofar region and on Masirah Island. Later, too, came the discovery of oil, though in no immensely rich deposits.

This relationship with the person of the Sultan was to continue with his son, Sultan Qaboes, an Oxford graduate, who ousted his despotic father in a 1970 palace coup after the failure of several assassination attempts by other opponents of the outdated regime. It was even to survive Britain's official withdrawal from East of Suez. Salilah, a regular posting for RAF personnel, was handed over to the Sultan's control in March 1977. At the same time the RAF withdrew from Masirah. Rumours that the US Air Force was taking over the island airfield were given only a qualified denial. Air controllers employed by the American airline Pan-Am took over operational control on behalf of the Sultan's authorities.

The Sultan's army was commanded by Major-General Kenneth Perkins, and about five hundred British officers still served under him even after the closure of these residual pockets of a quasi-secret British presence. Over one hundred were seconded from British Army units for service in Oman. Most were under direct contract as private individuals, 'screened and recommended', to the Sultan's government. In five years the number of Arab officers increased from fifteen honorary ranks to three hundred and fifty trained professionals. The old Sultan did not trust Arab military men. His personal bodyguard was paralleled by a palace guard of Muslims from the Indian state of Hyderabad.

This nebulous arrangement with the closed land of Muscat and Oman highlights the hypocrisy of statements made by Mr Denis Healey, then Minister of Defence, over an offer from the wealthy oil sheiks to pay the full £25 million support costs of keeping British forces in the Gulf bases of Bahrein and Sharjah. He confirmed Britain's rejection of their offer during a television interview in acid terms, responding to a well-meaning and reasonable offer with comments that British forces were not to be hired as mercenaries or white slaves. Britons already in the employ of the rulers were naturally outraged. A typical comment was made by Mr Stacey Barham, the police chief of Abu Dhabi, who said, 'We've been begging the Germans to pay support costs of the Rhine Army for years. Now they have oil the sheiks can afford to pay for us to see them through the upheavals of development. This is one place where Britain is still liked, respected and needed.'

The rulers themselves maintained polite silence on Mr Healey's uncalled-for rudeness, and went ahead with plans to buy weapons and hire the men to command their use. Naturally they turned first to Britain. In the words of an Arab notable, 'Britain is . . . Britain. It is our second homeland.'

The outer reception rooms of the rambling fortified palace, yet to be replaced by a marvel of modern architectural and technological splendour, were crammed when I went to keep an appointment with Sheik Zayad, then labelled the richest man in the world. Silk-suited businessmen from Lebanon, Europe and America mingled with sandalled tribesmen clutching ancient rifles.

Sheik Zayad wore ordinary Bedouin robes and smoked the traditional Bedouin pipe with a bowl scarcely bigger than an acorn. We sipped aromatic coffee. He talked softly of his hopes for a bright future for the peoples of the Gulf, evading the specific problems facing them, refusing to be drawn into any comment on Britain's withdrawal other than to hope that traditional friendship would remain and even grow stronger.

The commander of the embryo Abu Dhabi Defence Force, Lieutenant-Colonel Tug Wilson, a bluff Yorkshire veteran of RAF wartime bomber command, was appalled at British withdrawal. His desk was piled with brochures for guns, tanks, aircraft, hoverplanes and coastal launches. He had reckoned he had till about 1975 to build up the three arms of an adequate defence force.

In the seven years from 1968 to 1975 the population of the Trucial States bounded further – from two hundred thousand to six hundred thousand. Ten per cent of the Arab population were born in the area, but only one per cent of the local Arabs were employed in the new labour force.

The lessons of Kuwait and its immense internal security problem were well taken. The alien majority in the Gulf's population is widely cosmopolitan. Recruiting for labour was orientated towards the Muslim workers of Pakistan, desperate for well-paid jobs, to leaven a more potentially explosive mix of Palestinians, Jordanians, Lebanese and Persians. Today the Urdu language of North India is heard more often than Arabic. Pakistan was also an alternative to Britain for hired military expertise. Officers, modelled on the Sandhurst pattern, air force pilots and ground staff, mingle easily in the Gulf's new military forces with former regular officers of the British army and the RAF. By 1975 the Abu Dhabi Defence Force was swollen to 25,000 – almost equal with the native-born population – equipped with sophisticated military toys like Mirage fighters, anti-aircraft missiles.

By comparison to this military super-power Dubai's armed forces of about 3000 strength is in a minor league. The joint Union Defence Force, heirs of the Trucial Oman Scouts, remains at the old figure of 3000.

The defeat of the revolutionary regime of South Yemen in the Oman war, plus the financial adherence of the Gulf rulers to the Arab struggle against Israel, have contributed to continued stability. Early ideas of a grand federation embracing the seven Trucial States with Bahrein and Qatar quickly broke down. Bahrein and Qatar each became sovereign members of the United Nations when their treaty relationship with Britain was formally ended in 1971. The seven smaller states papered over tribal rivalries, formed the United Arab Emirates, and gained joint membership of the United Nations. But all seven developed separate police and defence forces, and there is much bickering along traditional tribal lines beneath the diplomatic surface. Sheik Zayad's immense wealth, even more his powerful military muscle, seem likely to perpetuate his presidency of the new nation.

In the end there were no echoes of the bitter recriminations of the South Arabian sheiks. No observable chaos was left behind to add to the scars of crash industrial development and brash modernization. No bloodshed erupted. Officials of the British Government, representatives of the Queen, hundreds of British businessmen and workers were accorded honoured places at ceremonies to inaugurate the new status of Bahrein, Qatar and the United Arab Emirates as fully responsible for their own destinies.

PART TWO
The Aftermath

24 The Oil Weapon

Rulers of the new oil bonanza lands of the lower Gulf studied the lessons of Kuwait's high wire walk to survival as they faced up to being left to look after themselves in a wolfish world ravenous for their oil or their cash.

Unlike Kuwait they were far removed geographically from the explosive heartland of the Palestine question. They had also minimized the fifth column risks of Palestinians mingling like Mao's fishes in their swollen populations by drawing labour and skills from many diverse lands.

But like Kuwait they found themselves impelled willy-nilly towards greater involvement in postures and verbal sentiments on the thorny question of Israel. More and more they were called upon to put hard cash behind easy sentiments to buy off threats of revolutionary incitement of their mushrooming urban communities, and for diplomatic support by the Arab revolutionary socialist states, natural foes on any ideological level. They were forced aboard the Arab bandwagon in the 'ceaseless battle for Arab rights in Palestine'.

Use of Arab oil as a weapon loomed large as a potential danger during the Six Day War of June 1967. Till then the only blows against the flow of Arab oil to 'western backers of Israel' had little more than nuisance value to the international oil companies concerned, hurting Arab consumers more than anybody. These pinpricks came from Arab extremist gangs, defying their own revolutionary regimes in Iraq and Syria, to launch bomb attacks on vulnerable pipelines snaking across the open desert between the oilfields and the Mediterranean.

As hubble-bubble pipe-dreams of a crushing victory were again dispelled in ignominious defeat on all three Arab fronts Arab pride was salvaged by characteristic self-delusion. The Arabs were convinced that they were robbed of victory by the intervention of American and British air power. Nasser concocted the BIG LIE that the Egyptian air force was destroyed on the ground by treacherous attacks carried out by planes that flew in from the Western Desert, from the American air base at Wheelus Field in Libya. RAF planes were also alleged to have intervened from bases in Cyprus. King Hussein of Jordan, may his conscience find peace, lamely corroborated Nasser's allegations in a taped telephone recording.

This was to have wide repercussions: the overthrow of the Senussi monarchy in Libya, the expulsion of America from Wheelus, the emergence of the ideologically mixed up, generally deranged, Colonel Gaddafi among the crazed dictators.

More immediately President Aref of Iraq warned that his country's oil would be withheld from any consumer state that helped Israel even at the cost of setting fire to the oilfields. Kuwait dutifully announced similar intentions as its internal security forces were put on riot alert. These announcements were followed by a conference of all the Arab oil producers in Baghdad where President Aref presided. He urged them to warn the oil companies of sequestration if they failed to co-operate in an Arab embargo of states 'participating with Israel in Aggression against the Arabs'. He appealed to the Shah of Persia to cut vital supplies to Israel and warned international companies with operations in Iran that their interests in Arab countries would be sequestrated if they continued supplying Iranian oil to Israel. The conference, representing at that time a threat to the bulk of Britain's supplies and one third of total world production, established an action committee under the chairmanship of Iraqi oil minister, Abdel Sattar Ali Hussein.

The committee began by announcing that any country attempting to break an Egyptian naval blockade of Israel's supply port of Aqaba, approached via the Red Sea, would be regarded as aggressors requiring 'application of Arab oil measures'.

The oil workers in Kuwait, well used to empty words from the ruling family, defied the stringent labour laws and called a general strike to enforce the official Arab embargo on supplies to Britain and America. They called for a complete shut-off of oil production, the immediate dismissal of all American and British staff, and the withdrawal of sterling reserves from London and its transfer to Cairo.

This last held the real pinch of a determined Arab economic war from Britain's point of view. At that time Kuwait held £325 million in cash reserves, and a many times greater amount in its portfolio of sterling investments. This was undoubtedly what Sheik Jaber Al Ahmed had in mind when he told me, 'We have more economic and psychological weapons we can use in the battle to win ultimate victory. Britain and America will simply have to decide between maintaining their interests in the Arab world and

Russia carried out a test run of oil as a weapon as early as 1960. It used its own surplus oil production. With it they quietly neutralized the hitherto unchallenged domination of world markets and prices, supply and demand, by the Big Seven international oil companies of the West. It passed without any noticeable concern outside the highly confidential discussions of the powerful tycoons whose monopoly control of this vital lubricant of Western economy was clearly about to slip away. It meant that never again would international oil capital be able to bring a rogue producer government to heel as was so successfully done after the Iranian nationalization of Abadan. There the buying boycott of the world oil cartel reduced Iran's oil exports from 54 million tons the year before nationalization to 132,000 tons the year afterwards, producing economic chaos in Iran that brought the fall and imprisonment of Mossadegh.

The Soviet ploy was devilishly simple. In May 1960, Russia offered to supply India with oil at 14 per cent below the Western price. Oil companies reacted by cutting prices for Middle East oil – arrogantly neglecting to consult or even advise the producer governments whose national revenues they thereby reduced overnight. This was a massive blow to Arab pride as well as to Arab pockets.

Iraq's dictator General Kassem, who leaned heavily on Soviet advice, invited representatives of the producer nations to Baghdad to discuss the situation. Iran, Venezuela, Saudi Arabia and Kuwait responded by sending their most senior oil experts. It was at this meeting that the Organization of Petroleum Exporting Countries (OPEC) was formed as a producer's cartel.

The aim was to present a united front so that the great combine of oil companies would not be able to play off one against another as happened after the Abadan affair. Its shattering success is reflected in today's oil prices – a matter of deepest concern to all who buy petrol, plastics, fertilizers and the many other by-products of this glutinous black liquid more precious than any other geological product not excluding gold.

Saudi Arabia's representative at this crucially historic meeting, a watershed in oil affairs with all its immense ramifications, was Sheik Abdullah Tariki, King Saud's Minister of Oil Affairs. Educated as a lawyer in America, he was to air his anti-company views too often and too openly, and was fortunately repladce in that key post. His successor was Sheik Ahmen Zaki Yamani, a name later to become a household word (to the fullest literary extent) because of his power over the purses of every family in the developed world. Sheik Yamani was to emerge from the later traumas of the four-fold price increase to combat pricing policies which took Soviet interests a great leap forward as the Western world was faced with perils of economic collapse.

Sheik Tariki in the meantime moved to Beirut and set up offices as an oil consultant. There he began preaching the potential of oil as a weapon against Israel. He chose a Congress of Arab lawyers held in the then Jordanian-controlled half of Jerusalem in November 1965, to make a penetrating analysis.

It went unnoticed at the time, partly because the Arab penchant for censorship was more developed in Jordan than anywhere else in the Arab world. (The King Hussein image was made in London, taken up by the American and European media, Arab romantics and bemused women interviewers, not by discerning visitors to Jordan.) In any case Tariki was way ahead of accepted thinking at that time. Oil autocrats left technology and finance to Western experts and concentrated on spending revenues for their own immediate pleasure. Tariki was written off as a radical.

Tariki told the lawyers, a profession more at the heart of politics in the Middle East than anywhere else, 'Arabs are in a strong bargaining position to exert economic and political pressure to force countries supporting Israel to think twice. Israel cannot make war without Western help, but now more than ever before the West is prepared to accept a solution that avoids exposing Western interests to crisis.'

He went on, 'The American Seventh Fleet (then beginning a bombing offensive against North Vietnam) and the British fleet in the east secure their petroleum supplies at Bahrein, Ras Tannoura, Kuwait and Aden. They cannot afford to lose these Arab oil sources without exposing their strategy to danger and high costs.'

Tariki's teaching was not taken seriously in the West. The current philosophy, dating from the successful 'blacking' of Abadan oil after that refinery's sequestration by Mossadegh more than a decade earlier, was that the Middle East producers depended more on Western markets in order to sell their oil than the West needed Middle East oil. Where else could the Arabs sell their oil? The Communist Bloc was self-sufficient. Russia was an exporter of oil, often ready to undercut Arab oil prices.

Everything changed when all-out war came again in October 1973. While great battles raged on both banks of the Suez Canal, Arab oil ministers met in the Sheraton Hotel in Kuwait determined to act against the economies of countries acting as arsenals for Israel's fighting comeback after suffering grave reverses for the first time in the recurrent wars and clashes with her Arab neighbours. This time there was no easy self delusion in blaming scapegoats for Arab failings. This time there was much substance in the Arabs' firm belief that their armies were robbed of victory by America's urgent replacement of Israeli planes shot down in droves by the new tactical use of Russian Sam Seven infantry missiles. America also airlifted new tanks to replace heavy battlefield losses due to the same Soviet missiles. Russia's equivalent air lift of replacement weapons to the Syrian army was considered irrelevant, of course, as any justification for the American action.

The Kuwait meeting took two measures that had immediate effects on Western economies, forcing immediate fuel-saving campaigns like ceilings on car speeds for the first time. Restrictions ranging from reduced heating of offices to slower cruising speeds for airliners were also introduced.

The first measure was what was then considered a swingeing increase in the price of crude oil – up by 17 per cent.

The Arab states of the Gulf, driven by anger, thus fell in with greedy Iranian pressures for increased prices. Then, as later and more blatantly, the Shah's immense royalties barely covered the vast expenditures on his ostentatious revelries, his genuine social and economic developments and reforms, but above all his highly sophisticated, astronomically costly military machine.

The second measure was to induce Saudi Arabia, deeply embarrassed by its close business links with the United States, to embargo oil supplies to its American partner. This involved cutting back production in the ARAMCO oilfields by 10 per cent, the amount of Saudi oil (600,000 barrels a day) shipped directly to America. This amounted to only about one-twentieth of America's vast consumption from many sources, only one-sixth of which came at that time from Middle East wells. But in Europe, as American purchasers shopped around to make up the difference in other oil markets, the price of oil went beyond the straight 17 per cent increase imposed on Gulf oil.

Thus the oil weapon was launched at last – by ten men in a plush modern hotel room, all in traditional Arab dress as invariably worn by their Kuwaiti hosts, all carrying a small fortune in gold and jewels on their fingers and wrists, all so seething with anger at the West that they were unable to show normal Arab courtesy to the lobbying world's press.

It seemed inconceivable to me, even feeling the heat of their anger at first hand, that they would continue long on a course so damaging to the West, fountain of their riches, and so encouraging to the Soviet objective of toppling the capitalist system of which they were so much a part. But, as everybody knows, they did.

It must be stated that the Arabs had a fair argument, as primary producers, for a bigger share in the profits exacted at the petrol pump in most Western consumer countries. The international oil companies had long kept oil so cheap that governments in consumer countries were deriving much greater revenues from taxes on its sale as motor fuel than the producer countries were getting in royalties. Even then prices were low enough to permit vast wastage and misuse of a limited natural resource in affluent communities where little or no thought was given to the needs (not to mention ecological questions) of future generations. There had long been a case for the big oil companies to improve the producer state's share of the vast profits once the initial exploration and development capital was recouped. It was not realistic to dismiss such ideas with the truism that the Arabs were getting more return than they knew what to do with as it was, merely for pitching their tents on top of riches they were incapable of bringing to fruition.

But the 17 per cent increase that shook the Western world in 1973 was only a beginning. The Arabs were then merely getting the bit of producer power between their teeth. Prices were later to be raised fourfold, bringing Britain to the brink of economic collapse, and the whole non-communist world its gravest financial crisis, still far from resolved. The accumulated Arab cash reserves from oil revenues rose rapidly, despite more economy-conscious consumers. These bank balances were to hit Britain harder still.

Kuwaitis, tutored by Lebanese bankers, were old hands at playing the currency markets with their cash floats. They profited by deals in sterling while British soldiers were sitting out in the blistering heat of the desert between their air-conditioned palaces and the booty-seeking Iraqis during the annexation threat of 1961. When sterling was floated they and the Saudis used the London money market as a high stakes casino in which a system backed by sufficiently high chips could hardly lose. Such immense sums were involved that Arab syndicates were able to manipulate the rate, buying back when the rate dropped from their own earlier selling.

Kuwait Government balances were withdrawn from sterling when the rate dropped to $2·20 to the pound, sending it plunging like a stone below $2. Saudi Arabia sold out when it reached $2·17. Britain spun deeper and deeper into financial and economic crisis, teetering on total ruin.

While the Gulf Sheiks made more and more money, the goods and services from Britain came cheaper and cheaper, despite inflationary price increases, with each delivery. The former paramount power was pauperized at the hands of erstwhile Arab protégés.

There were other factors in Britain's financial bankruptcy. The irresponsible sabotage of the Western financial system by the Arabs brought the British malaise to crisis more rapidly. One of these factors was a loss of confidence, a loss of pride amounting to shame for the greatness of the past. This was at the core of Britain's abdication of responsibility in Aden and the Gulf.

But for that withdrawal of protection the Gulf rulers, already constipated with oil revenues, might well have listened to wiser counsels instead of impetuously agreeing to advance the Soviet interest more devastatingly than the Kremlin conspirators dare do themselves.

In the mid-seventies, for reasons expounded in the next chapter, Saudi Arabia moved into a protective relationship with America little different in practice to the relationship Britain ended with Bahrein in 1971.

This, in fact, signalled a stop to the unthinking misuse of oil as a weapon serving Soviet objectives of disruption and world revolution.

From that time the Saudi oil minister, Sheik Zaki Yamani, campaigned against further sharp price increases in the councils of the Arab oil producers and split the wider OPEC cartel. This more considered attitude undoubtedly prevented still higher oil prices that might have dealt death blows to the West's fragile climb back towards economic viability, and opened West Europe to communist takeover.

25 Back to Piracy

Meanwhile the very existence of Aden was all but forgotten in the outside world. Its name was mentioned occasionally in connection with a hijacked airliner or came to brief and cursory attention as refuge and lair of international terrorists.

The first coup attempt against Aden's first ruler after the departure of the British, President Qahtan Ashaabi, came in March 1968, when the new republic was just over three months old. It came, as might have been expected, from an army leadership appalled at the chaos which the ardent proponents of 'scientific Marxism' had by that time produced. The coup leaders, including the former Deputy Commissioner of Police, Brigadier Abdullah Saleh Aulaqi, promoted Chief of the Armed Forces, agreed to order the troops back to barracks after an undertaking by President Ashaabi that he would curb his fanatical extremists. Ashaabi's prestige as leader of the triumphant National Liberation Front was already diminished by whispers that he had sold out to the British by negotiating a peaceful withdrawal in exchange for a pittance in compensation for a hundred and twenty-nine years of colonial oppression. Ashaabi had demanded £100 million. Britain had finally agreed to hand over a sum of £1,500,000, mostly to cover civil service pensions.

Threats of retaliation by nationalizing the British Petroleum refinery were bandied about, but wiser counsels had prevailed with the argument that the refinery was the only continuing source of major income that was left. Hence the British Embassy remained the solitary target. It had only squatters-rights to an area of twenty-five acres occupied during the illegal regime. Subsequently the embassy was reduced to similar accommodation to that provided for South Yemen's London embassy in Cromwell Road, and had to move to a modest villa in Khormaksar.

Ashaabi's attempts to check the wilder elements among his supporters merely won him scorn. Dissidents among the forty-one members of the Central Committee denounced the President as a tool of the bourgeois remnant. The leader of the far left faction was Salim Ali Rubei, close comrade of Ashaabi throughout the struggle for power. He was the man known to British Intelligence as 'Suleiman', one of the most active terrorists, believed to have personally killed several Britons. Forewarned of his impend-

co-operation with the refugee army column and to claim back the equipment. He described the refugees as conspirators.

Relations between the ancient state of Yemen and its southern neighbour, known in British days as the 'occupied south', were strained from the first days of Aden's independence because of the continued presence in Taiz of Abdullah al-Asnag and a colony of FLOSY survivors.

President Ashaabi, before he emerged as NLF leader, had himself served as 'Minister for the Occupied South' in earlier Nasserite governments in Sanaa. But the withdrawal of Egyptian forces was followed by a series of government changes in Sanaa, each more moderate than its predecessor until former royalists came to share power with more moderate republicans. The fervour as well as the tide of Arab revolution was running cold. Saudi money, arms and influence returned to Sanaa. Relations between the two Yemens plunged lower than they had been in British times.

In 1969 the North Yemen government blamed Ashaabi for backing an attempted coup by Marxist hotheads led by Colonel Abdul Raqeeb, a hero of the successful defence of Sanaa against a royalist offensive during the long civil war. He had been exiled to Aden five months before, but his body was found in the ruins of a house in Sanaa which government forces had stormed in operations to suppress the coup. 1990 - N/S Yemen merge.

Union remains an elusive dream, still shattered by ideological splits of rivals factions in Aden and Sanaa. The Sanaa government demonstrated its claim to the south in 1975 by appointing Abdullah al-Asnag Foreign Minister of the Yemen Arab Republic. The unstated inference is that its southern territories are temporarily under control of a revolutionary faction.

This continuing clash of Yemenis spilled blood in London at Easter 1977 when Abdullah a-Hajari, a former North Yemen Prime Minister of pro-Saudi policies, was assassinated by a lone gunman – in identical tactics to those used by Aden's 'assassin of Steamer Point'.

However, back in 1968 Ashaabi had more pressing worries than continuing support on his border for FLOSY interventionists. He was quietly ousted from power after just over eighteen months as his country's first President on 22 June 1969. The reinstated extremists who had attempted the armed rebellion a year before took over in a bloodless committee coup.

Salim Ali Rubei, the former terrorist killer codenamed 'Suleiman', became chairman of a three-man Presidency Council. The following November, on the third anniversary of independence, the appointment of a Supreme People's Council of one hundred and one members was announced.

South Yemen's one-party state became a closed land. The extremist regime introduced land and property reforms with a ruthlessness only paralleled by the horrific regime in Cambodia. It fought off attempted incursions from its FLOSY rivals as well as from traditional leaders like the old Sherif of Beihan with Saudi Arabian financial backing. It maintained internal power by murderous police state methods. East German advisers helped set up a new internal security system on Gestapo lines. Hundreds whose loyalty was so much as doubted simply disappeared. One was the chief magistrate of the Supreme Court, bold enough in the early days to release political detainees because they had committed no crime under the Criminal Code. Thousands were held in political re-education centres.

South Yemen's confident assumptions that it would rapidly succeed in spreading its revolutionary politics into the oil lands of the Gulf were thwarted. The long insurgency into Oman's Dhofar region on South Yemen's north-easterly borders ended in triumph for the Sultan's multi-national armed forces when the frontier was effectively sealed at the end of 1975. In the final campaigns of the nine years' Dhofar War the Shah sent a hard-hitting expeditionary force of 2500 elite troops with sophisticated air support. This Persian military presence in the Arabian Peninsula, uncertainly welcomed by Riyadh, condoned even by Cairo, shows just how internationally isolated South Yemen had become.

General poverty replaced widespread prosperity. In the financial year 1974–5 estimates put revenue, mainly from the British Petroleum refinery, at £18 million. The bustling free port of British days is replaced by severe import controls, and passenger liners and even coastal shipping prefer to steer clear of its unpredictable bureaucracy. The port operates old-fashioned lightering systems with no modern container facilities or transport vehicles and roads for heavy load distribution. Hodeida, and even Jedda in Saudi Arabia, have taken over Aden's traditional entrepot role for the Yemen hinterland.

There is no encouragement for foreign investment despite enormous capital requirements for development. All private ownership has been abolished. Even the mosques have been nationalized, and Mullah priests are paid a state salary and have to submit sermons to censorship. Under an anti-fraternization law citizens of South Yemen were even banned from talking with foreigners. In the Little Aden refinery this ban was lifted during office hours, but in the company club the remaining British and their Yemeni colleagues sit at opposite ends of the bar.

The repair of the Egyptian oil refineries at Suez brought an end of full capacity production which the temporary boom of refining Egyptian crude had brought to the Little Aden oil town. By 1976 operations were reduced to little more than a care and maintenance level, and the British Petroleum Company gave a year's notice of closure to the South Yemen Government. The Aden authorities protested and pressed the company to stay, but there was nothing they could do about it but accept the refinery as a gift. The company invoked an agreement, providing for the building of the refinery at the request of the British Colonial Government, twenty years before. This specifically allowed the company to close down if the refinery operations became unviable. The huge complex, built in the mid-fifties at a cost of £44 million, formally passed into South Yemen government ownership on 1 May 1977 without so much as a mention in the British news media.

South Yemen paid only for moveable assets – sold at a price the company chooses not to reveal – after negotiations with the South Yemen oil minister, a former BP trainee. Under the agreement forty-four key British personnel remain at their posts until Yemeni replacements have been trained. British Petroleum retained its BP bunkering service company although it was handling only about one-tenth of its old business.

The inevitable pressures of economic reality began to force some lifting of this blanket isolation in the early summer of 1977. Saudi Arabia and Kuwait agreed to process crude in the Little Aden refinery, demanding as part of the price South Yemen's cessation of support for insurgency in neighbouring Oman. These two Arab lands, under traditional sheikly rule so detested by NLF doctrine, have also started a joint bunkering company. Saudi Arabia has even opened an embassy in Aden.

The South Yemen army occupies the one-time BP general manager's mansion, a splendid modern villa set high amid a wasteland of rock and sand and sea. With a refrigerator in every bedroom it was perfect for an officers' mess.

L.S.–N

Close by Little Aden the British cemetery at Silent Valley is unmolested, kept tidy by a caretaker.

Beyond it, in luxurious military housing at Falaise Camp, completed just before the British withdrawal, the Cubans are lodged as honoured guests. The £50,000 church of revolutionary design is used as a lecture hall for guerrilla war tactics. The Japanese Red Army also have instructors there. Aden is used for planning liaison with Arab operations.

As an international pariah South Yemen offers an ideal training ground for urban terrorists of many nationalities who attend instructional courses there. Among rare guests at the Crescent Hotel are terrorists like the five German anarchists released from jail and flown to Aden in March 1975 with £20,000 in Deutschmarks – the ransom the Baader-Meinhof gang extorted for the release of a kidnapped West German politician. A year before that five terrorists of the People's Front for the Liberation of Palestine took over the Japanese embassy in Kuwait and demanded that four comrades be brought from Singapore in a Japanese Airlines plane, which then took all nine of them to Aden.

These direct escapes to safe refuge were not encouraged because they brought publicity to Aden's role in the web of conspiracy for world revolution. Most freed terrorists made their way to Aden via Beirut after last sightings in places like Libya and Iraq. Since the Lebanese holocaust destroyed the teeming refugee camps around Beirut as safe havens for low-lying terrorists the main route to Aden switched via Entebbe in Uganda.

The PFLP had played a helpful training role in the campaign against the British forces in Aden, even more in the NLF's internecine struggle with the 'bourgeois FLOSY' terrorists for control of the abandoned territory.

The politics of the Palestinian Marxists conformed closely to the thinking of the revolutionary theorists in power in Aden. Their objectives – the destruction of Israel, the overthrow of the feudal and bourgeois Arab governments, world revolution – were shared by the South Yemen leaders.

The military leader of the PFLP, Wadi Hadad, uses Aden during the planning and rehearsal stage of operations. The infamous Carlos, projected as the archetypal terrorist of the age by the west's image-building media, is known to spend much time in Aden. The Beirut headquarters of the political founder of this avenging, Marxist extremist movement, George Habash, was long considered too vulnerable to Israeli interference or infiltration to serve as a location for the months of careful planning involved in some of the more spectacular operations.

South Yemen officials have attempted international operations of terrorist violence themselves. In the summer of 1976 an attempt was made on the life of a noted Aden exile, Mohamed Haitham. His car was ambushed in the centre of Cairo. He was wounded, his chauffeur killed by gunfire.

Egyptian police accused a consul at the South Yemen embassy in Cairo of providing a silencer for the murder weapon. The Egyptian manager of the South Yemen Airlines office in Cairo and a Palestinian were arrested, tried and hanged.

In a few short years the wheel turned full circle in Aden – back to the state of poverty and piracy which the British found in 1839.

Piracy in its modern form of terrorist blackmail and extortion has found a natural habitat there. Historically, as mentioned earlier, the word 'assassin' springs from a sect of political killers founded by a South Arabian fanatic a thousand years ago.

The People's Republic of South Yemen, outcast even in its own Arab world, has cordial relations only with the Communist countries and their Third World client states. It is an old and good truism that you can tell the character of a person by the friends he chooses. Likewise with the motives and ethics of the elitist cliques who claim to carry the banner for ordinary people everywhere.

26 Zone of Soviet Peace

A slogan shaping an Arcadian dream of the Indian Ocean as 'an ocean of peace' began in New Delhi, capital of a land that fought three full-scale wars and countless skirmishes with its neighbour in its first twenty-five years of independence. It was echoed from the African shores, notably by Tanzania's President Julius Nyerere, a political academic widely respected as a sort of African Pandit Nehru.

It came just at the moment the British government, under left-wing pressures, was seeking ways of making impressive cuts in defence spending. It also coincided with desires to shed untidy remnants of inherited imperial responsibility in Aden and the Gulf. Hence the idea of a neutral ocean played some part in the decision to withdraw British forces, and the consequent creation of a power vacuum in the area.

This call for a nuclear-free zone also had influence in Washington long before President Carter brought his new broom to US foreign policy. The old US forward policy was already a casualty of post-Vietnam yearnings for neo-isolationism when the administration changed. Developing plans in the Pentagon to replace the British presence in the immediate area East of Suez were swept under desk blotters. Discreet improvements to naval and air installations, leased from Britain on a group of mid-ocean coral islands called Diego Garcia were delayed by Congressional Committee haggles over voting funds for 'new overseas involvements'.

No such inhibitions stood in the path of Soviet intentions. Ever since the shame of climbdown from Khrushchev's Cuban confrontation in 1962, when the US Navy forced the return of Soviet ships carrying nuclear rockets to its Caribbean satellite, Soviet military chiefs had given highest priority to plans for a global naval capability. The British withdrawal from Aden and the Gulf was the opening they needed. In 1968, only months after the British quit Aden, a squadron of Soviet warships 'showed the flag' in eight countries bordering the Indian Ocean. By the early seventies a Soviet Fleet of thirty-one warships, using South Yemen's Socotra Island as a regular anchorage, dominated the oil tanker seaway to Europe and America and the vast ocean depths where nuclear armed submarines can lurk with increased security from detection and counter-strike. This blatant flouting of Soviet muscle brought cheers and jubilant welcome for the ships and their crews from littoral countries like Iraq, South Yemen, Somalia, Tanzania and Mozambique.

To more stable countries like Kenya the presence of a newly emerging European expansionist power off her shores added considerably to fears for security along frontiers dominated by Marxist neighbours. In the earliest years of independence the Western-orientated regime of the former guerrilla fighter, President Kenyatta, had defeated an insurgency in northern provinces claimed by Somalia. The unpredictable Idi Amin of Uganda was also threatening to conquer a 'land bridge' for direct access to a supply port on the Indian Ocean.

Both Somalia and Uganda were receiving military aid, advisers as well as arms, from the Soviet Union far in excess of rational defence requirements.

India, with a submarine fleet provided and trained by the Soviet Union, managed to evade Moscow efforts to share the east-coast naval base at Vishakhapatnam which the Soviets had helped to modernize and enlarge. Ceylon's Marxist-leaning government, under pressures from New Delhi, also withheld the fine anchorage at Trincomalee, wartime base of the British East India fleet.

At the same time there was a continuing chorus of protest at American violations of the Ocean Peace Zone. A 'familiarization tour' of the Gulf by the US aircraft carrier *Constellation,* escorted by two guided missile cruisers in 1974, brought organized anti-imperialist rallies out on the streets in Dar-es-Salaam, Mogadishu and Bombay. This demonstration of US naval muscle was necessitated by the denigrating comparisons Arabs had been making between the tiny ships based on Bahrein and the mightier looking vessels flying the Red Flag which frequently sailed within sight of their shores. But the main chorus of protest was aimed at queering the Pentagon's pitch in the corridors of Congress and the lobbies of Westminster. Its target was a conspiracy among 'cold war warriors' of the west to set up a nuclear strike base at Diego Garcia, right in the middle of the Ocean Peace Zone.

In the vanguard of protest were organs of the Soviet information media, whose editorials were widely reproduced from handouts to the state press and radio throughout the Third World. As is well known, to borrow a phrase beloved of compilers of Soviet pronouncements of self-righteousness, the Soviet forces were launched into the Indian Ocean solely for the defence of peace-loving peoples.

Diego Garcia is the largest of a group of coral atolls designated British Indian Ocean Territory. It is 1200 miles almost due south of the tip of India, slightly nearer to Kenya than to Western Australia. An agreement for the United States to share the RAF facilities there was initiated by the Wilson government in 1966 at the time the decision was made to jettison any idea of maintaining a base at Aden. The lease agreement was in fact part of a cut-price deal for the supply of American Polaris missiles to the Royal Navy.

The Diego Garcia lease was confirmed by the Heath Government in 1972, and has been under frequent attack by party left-wingers since Labour returned to power. Concern has, however, been somewhat muted, largely due to inward-looking parliamentary agenda that in recent years have precluded real debate on such irrelevances as foreign affairs.

Britain's withdrawal from the tiny naval base at Juffair on Bahrein Island worried the Pentagon chiefs. Tankers under contract to the US Department of Defence were loading around two-and-a-half million tons of aviation and other fuels from the American-owned Bapco refinery each year. The small ship facilities were quietly taken over by the US Navy, which had become an increasingly frequent visitor to the base as the British prepared to leave. It became headquarters of a new Middle East Force responsible to the Commander-in-Chief, US Forces in Europe. It is still there despite temporary threats of expulsion during the 1973 Arab-Israeli War, and following Mr Henry Kissinger's indiscretions about possible American military intervention if vital supplies from the Gulf oilfields became critically threatened.

Meanwhile the Soviet Navy had found itself a major permanent base that saved the enormous logistical effort behind maintaining its initial Indian Ocean fleet from the Soviet Far East or around the Cape. Earlier plans for Russia's first warm water port – the dream of the old czars – to be sited at Um Qasar in Iraq were abandoned immediately after the 1968 announcement of Britain's phased withdrawal from the Gulf within three years.

The politically indefinable Marxist-Leninist-split-Baathist-Arab nationalist government of Iraq had entered into a Treaty of Friendship and Co-operation with the Soviet Union. Among other states to sign similar documents were South Yemen and Somalia. The Aden regime appeared too unpredictable even for Moscow in terms of critical investment, and the decision to site the Soviet's forward base in the Indian Ocean settled on Berbera in the Somali People's Republic. Berbera, village-size capital of former British Somaliland, sits on the Horn of Africa immediately opposite Aden, facing and commanding the entrance to the Strait of Bab al-Mandeb and the Red Sea.

The Somalis, among the most energetic people of the area, now have the largest armoured forces in Black Africa. The 1969 strength of the army was 12,000. By 1976 this had doubled to about 25,000.

Beginning in 1971 with two moored ships, one a barracks, the other a repair ship, the base was developed rapidly as a base for a major fleet. There are huge storage depots, arsenals and repair yards. A 12,000-foot runway is being extended. It operates regular flights between the base and the Soviet homeland. The long-range reconnaissance plane TU 95 is based there. So is an anti-submarine squadron of IL 38s. The defences include missile sites.

The base played a major role in the Soviet Navy's first global exercise in 1975, a clear demonstration that no part of the world is now beyond Soviet power to intervene. The normal complement of about twenty fighting ships, plus 'naval associated shipping', includes five surface missile ships with patrol escorts, two submarines armed with cruise missiles, minesweepers, LST and amphibious craft. These ships give wide flexibility in operations, including support of insurgent forces for a beach landing. Most of its current energies are put into training. Intelligence reports indicate a low density of operations.

Its significant role is that it provides a permanent presence and an ever growing surge capability, the logistical framework for rapid build-up of strike power and reinforcements. Since the reopening of the Suez Canal sailings between Berbera and Soviet naval bases in the Crimea are reduced to five or six days. The Western decision to help Egyptian authorities clear the canal was made on a calculation that diplomatic gains outweighed the evident military advantage that ensued for Moscow.

NATO has a unique spyhole on the Soviet base. As the British left the area the French moved in a squadron of three warships, including a missile frigate, to ensure uninterrupted access to the French colony at Djibouti, just a hundred and forty miles along the coast from the Soviet's Indian Ocean base at Berbera.

The French have an uncanny genius for getting away with activities in old colonies – and in arms testing and in circumventing trading embargoes – with none of the uproar from the Soviets and the Third World that invariably surrounds every Anglo-Saxon move. Nine thousand square miles of scrub on the African shore of the Strait of Bab al-Mandeb called French Somaliland was renamed The French Territory of the Afars and Issas in 1967 in Gallic dismissal of Somali claims to the port (railhead for the vast hinterland of Ethiopia) and its population of 81,000. The French counted on rival claims to the territory by Ethiopia and Somalia cancelling out determined opposition to their own practical arrangements. The French government blandly announced that its newly expanded naval base and its Foreign Legion garrison would remain after the territory gained its nominal independence in the summer of 1977.

While American plans to counter the massive Soviet build-up were harassed by Congressional reluctance to fund new foreign ventures, a diplomatic exercise was carried through to take account of Third World calls for an ocean neutral zone. America announced its willingness to negotiate an agreement with the Soviet Union for the mutual withdrawal of all foreign forces from the Indian Ocean area. This met with zero reaction from the Kremlin, and was soon overtaken by yet another crisis of Soviet expansion in the Southern Hemisphere.

This was the use of Cuban troops as catspaw for the Soviet military intervention that swung the Angola struggle in favour of its proteges of the MPLA. The racial hatred and fears of black and white in Africa were being exploited in a similar way to the Soviet meddling in the Arab-Israeli dispute. Brinkmanship was back with this demonstration of Soviet logistical support of the Cuban expeditionary force and its total dependence on Soviet naval and air capabilities. So much for two years of patient negotiations – and Soviet double-talk on human rights – that led to the documents so solemnly and hopefully signed at Helsinki, misleading so many in the West to attitudes of *détente*.

Meanwhile Pentagon planners were burrowing away with plans of their own aimed at countering Russian power. Many things are done by governmental bodies that never come to the attention of voters in open societies as in the closed societies of the communist bloc and the elitist or gangster-led societies of most countries of the Third World. Even in America, most open of all open societies, there are so many varied channels of activity vying for attention that much goes unnoticed. The art of the governmental *fait accompli* is well practised.

In Britain officials are much less subject to public awareness. The phrase 'in committee' is synonymous with secret in the parlance of local councils as well as regional and national bodies. Public officials in the higher echelons work under a cloak of inbred denial, often bordering on contempt of the public's right to know. There is also subtle application of direct censorship in the form of 'D-notices' covering the publication of information involving national security; a term capable of wide and varied interpretation.

Quietly then, almost by sleight of hand, the Pentagon went about its business of countering the Soviet expansion of power into the Indian Ocean.

Every concept of strategic counter balance in the southern seas came back to the key value of a major base in Diego Garcia. Nowhere else in the world was more remote from the nearest population. The scattered atolls of the Maldive Republic and its 130,000 population (site of another deserted RAF staging post on the island of Gan) is nine hundred miles to the north. The nearest large centres of population are well over a thousand miles away. Diego Garcia's own indigenous population of 1151 was moved 1200 miles to Mauritius on payment by Britain of £650,000 for their resettlement. The last of them left when the Copra plantations closed in 1971.

It was ideally sited as a discreet counter to the Soviet naval build-up in the Indian Ocean; perfect as a base for nuclear strike submarines and anti-submarine air patrols. From the vast depths of the Arabian Sea, in the north-west areas of the great ocean, undersea-launched missiles could reach Leningrad and beyond.

Seabees – the pioneer corps of the US Navy – made up most of the 1300 American personnel who have taken over from a token force of twenty-five British servicemen. The old 8000-foot runway was extended to 12,000 feet, the lagoon dredged, a re-fuelling pier built. Signals and other electronic installations have been what is tacitly termed 'upgraded', storage facilities are on a huge scale. On 1977 estimates the US will have spent $175 million on the base by 1980.

Its main present capability is deployment of units of the Pacific Fleet into the Indian Ocean to contest Soviet Naval domination of the key areas two thousand miles to the north. Its surge capability, like that of the Soviet base at Berbera, is considerable.

A quite unexpected threat to the security of the Soviet base at Berbera developed in the summer of 1977. The tide was running too strongly the Soviet way in the Horn of Africa, presenting the Kremlin with a difficult diplomatic problem.

The leaders of Ethiopia's bloody and far-from-stabilized revolution turned to Russia for arms, and the Soviet's willingness to take another client caused much consternation to the Somali landlords of the base at Berbera. Not only were the Ethiopians and Somalis rival claimants to Djibouti, newly emerging into the hazardous state of independence from French colonial rule, but

Somalia laid claim to the vast Ogaden region of Ethiopia. It was to back these claims that the Somalis initially allowed the Soviets facilities in exchange for arms and training.

Reluctant to pass up the chance of embracing this considerable new defector from Western influence the Soviets sent the Cuban leader, Fidel Castro, to the Somali capital of Mogadishu and to Aden with a sensational solution to all the problems of the area. This was no less than the formation of a mini-Soviet Union of Ethiopia, Somalia and South Yemen. The idea was received coldly in Mogadishu, with incredulity in Aden. This was the first sign of the Soviet weakness of over-extension in Africa. This weakness was already bringing a resurgence of pro-Western ideas in the Middle East where Soviet domination in Cairo and Khartoum met dramatic reverses.

The Shah's Iran provides a nagging worry to the Soviet military chiefs. It is a pocket of volatile power in territorial dispute with their client state, Iraq, and across their lines of communication. They count on internal events inside Iran to take care of this problem in due course – a strange attitude over a country whose internal security matches the Soviet Union's own measures of repression in its police aspects.

The Shah controls powerful military forces equipped with the best weapons money can buy – at an incidental cost of crippling the capitalist economies which supply them because of Iran's insatiable budgetary demands for OPEC to agree to higher prices. Much of Iran's expenditure on sophisticated arms – 17 per cent of national income compared with 3 to 6 per cent by major NATO countries – is recycled into the British economy via custom for the arms (Chieftain tanks especially) and aerospace industries. But the inflationary sabotage of the ordinary family budget in Britain and other countries is already inflicted.

Like every Persian the Shah nurses resentment over the joint occupation by British and Soviet forces in World War Two when he was installed on his ousted father's throne. Against that and the further humbling of his country by the Western oil companies during the lengthy Abadan crisis – when he himself was briefly forced to seek refuge abroad – he determined to make his country a power in its own right.

His ambition was to restore some of the glories of Iran's imperial past, and for himself to emerge as a King-of-Kings (the literal translation of his title Shahinshah, never abbreviated to mere Shah in Iran) to be reckoned with.

He saw his opportunity when the British announced their policy of withdrawal from its traditional role in the Persian Gulf. He saw Iran as Britain's successor as the paramount power. He found that he had competitors. Not only was there the sudden and rapidly consolidated emergence of Soviet naval power throughout the Gulf and far beyond, there was also a mature, realistic partnership evolving between the royal rulers of Saudi Arabia and their mighty protector, the United States.

It became clear by 1977 that the pivot of American military thinking in the area had quietly switched to Saudi Arabia, the world's richest country, source of immense oil reserves. It also has a tiny, mostly thinly dispersed population – little for Mao's little fishes of malcontent to swim in. Saudi Arabia's population of an estimated seven millions occupies a vast desert peninsula of 927,000 square miles. Its strategic situation, too, is ideal – nicely buffered from contiguity with the Soviet periphery.

The relationship between the hard-headed Americans and the world-hardened heirs of the devil-may-care desert warriors, who conquered the vast area of the Arabian Peninsula by the sword less than a lifespan ago, changed significantly. The desert-robed playboys familiar in European and American casinos and night-clubs during King Saud's indulgent years slowly learned the perils of the tumultuous world outside their cloistered homeland, the Holy Land of Islam. They were chastened and disciplined during the ten years' reign of the late King Feisal, a sage, austere, dedicated ruler. They see their only chance of survival, other than joining their Swiss bank accounts in exile, with the Americans whose blatant oil imperialism often irked them. For families as rich as theirs, close links with the simmering Arab world beyond the desert horizons must be fatal. Revolutionary forces such as the Palestinian groups, more fanatical for full-scale, violent revolution than for righting injustices in Palestine, would sweep them aside without a moment's gratitude for their role as paymaster in the battle against Israel, should the Soviet imperialists succeed in driving the Americans and their allies out of the area.

The near collapse of West Europe's economy and recession in America shocked them into a second look at the use of oil as a weapon against Israel. This brought a startling new awareness of the Soviet double game of using Arabs to further its constant aim of revolutionary subversion of the West. They realized with shattering clarity that this aim, not justice for Palestinians, is the reason for cynical all-out backing of the Arabs against Israel, incidentally the only functioning, democratically elected socialist state in the Middle East until the 1977 election brought a frightened right-wing backlash. This Israeli fright was caused by developing new attitudes in America towards the old stereotype policy of unquestioning support against any risk of Israel's extermination.

This, itself, stemmed from the Saudis being persuaded by American advice that they can best help solve some of the problems of Palestine by working for a more sympathetic attitude towards the Arab point of view on Palestine. It seemed worth a try even before the arrival of the Carter regime opened up a whole new diplomatic ball game. Three decades of sterile, vengeful dreams of military reconquest and four punishing wars in efforts to fulfil them had left Israel more firmly established than ever, sitting on vast areas of indisputably Arab territory.

The Egyptian president, Anwar Sadat, was induced to share this review of basic Arab interests, and acted with astonishing boldness in expelling Soviet advisers in his more vulnerable position in the mainstream of explosive Arab politics. He used the Saudis as middlemen for arms purchases from the West.

North Yemen's moderate regime joined this new alignment of mutual Arab interest, having already reverted to American arms aid after twenty years as a Soviet customer in the merchandise of killing. Soviet designs on the Horn of Africa served as a spur. Similar considerations brought Sudan into this Saudi Arabian led group.

Even the moodily secretive regime in Damascus, with its own brand of Baathist pan-Arab socialism, began to open up. Syria dropped its erstwhile attitude that Israel's total military defeat was the only solution to the endemic Middle East problem.

Discreetly, Saudi Arabia's long relationship, through many ups and downs, with America, had developed into a protective and advisory alliance. The military aspect of this became apparent when the United States Corps of Engineers moved an entire divisional headquarters from Europe to the Saudi Arabian capital of Riyadh. Ostensibly, this was for closer supervision of a twenty-billion dollar programme of construction, including roads and airports, under a contract between the Saudi Arabian government and the US Department of Defence.

The power confrontation has switched in a novel way. The

struggle is now between power stemming from countless barrels of oil – and power from the barrels of revolutionary guns. In an area where money buys friends more persuasively than anywhere else, the Saudis, with their minuscule population, look like succeeding in buying the expulsion of dominant Soviet influence from the Arab world. By doing so they restore the superpower balance upset by the Soviet naval breakthrough into the Indian Ocean, and offset some of the worst consequences of Britain's abdication of power in that area.

They back Egypt's new independence of Russian aid with their tremendous financial resources. It was their wealth that brought an imposed, if uneasy, peace to tragic Lebanon. They bought off South Yemen's assistance to rebellion in Oman.

All this flows from their extra special relationship with the United States with its reverse flow of influence for more understanding sympathy in Washington for the Arabs' deep concern that Palestine must never be allowed to petrify as an unresolvable problem. This diplomatic offensive has been carried through with a new, unfaltering confidence born of the security of a home base under the firmest American protection.

The proud Saudi princes – some four thousand of them under the real leadership of King Khalid and some four of his closest relatives – would doubtless disdain any comparison with the petty sheikdoms of the Gulf. But this American role is no less a mantle of protection and worldly advice than that which Britain withdrew from the tiny Gulf states at the beginning of the decade.

Index